MERCE CUNNINGHAM

CREATIVE ELEMENTS

Choreography and Dance, 1997, Vol. 4(3)
Photocopying permitted by license only

Contents

Choreography and Dance, 1997, Vol. 4(3), p. 1
Photocopying permitted by license only

Introduction

Merce Cunningham reached the age of seventy-seven in 1996, an age at which many creative artists are content to rest on their laurels, or at least to leave behind whatever controversies they may have caused during their careers. Not so Cunningham. In the first place, his seventies have been a time of intense creativity in which he has choreographed as many as four new works a year. And Cunningham is as strongly committed as ever to the discovery of new ways of moving and of making movement, refusing to be hampered by the physical limitations that have come with age. Since 1991 every new work has been made at least in part with the use of the computer program Life Forms, which enables him to devise choreographic phrases that he himself would be unable to perform – and which challenge and develop the virtuosity of the young dancers in his company.

The essays collected in this number of *Choreography and Dance* have been written over the last few years. They deal with various aspects of the work of Merce Cunningham as seen both from the outside and the inside: Joan Acocella and Marilyn Vaughan Drown both discuss, from different viewpoints, the question of the content of his dances; Nelson Rivera chronicles the celebrated collaborations with visual artists in the late sixties; William Fetterman contributes an analysis of a fascinating but little known Cage-Cunningham collaboration, Cunningham's assumption of the role of conductor in Cage's *Concert for Piano and Orchestra*, 1958; John Holzaepfel, whose 1993 doctoral dissertation for the City University of New York deals with David Tudor's pioneering performances of experimental music in the fifties, concentrates on Tudor's work with the musical scores of the early repertory of the Cunningham Dance Company.

Gordon Mumma was one of the company musicians in the late sixties and early seventies, contributing such scores as *Mesa* for Cunningham's *Place* in 1966 and *Telepos* for *TV Rerun* in 1972; he traces the development of live electronic music, an important contribution of the Cunningham Company to contemporary music. Thecla Schiphorst, herself a choreographer as well as a computer scientist, is a member of the team that developed the LifeForms program at Simon Fraser University and has frequently traveled to New York to tutor Merce Cunningham in its use; she has thus an intimate knowledge of Cunningham's involvement with this technology. Finally, Elliot Caplan, filmmaker-in-residence at the Cunningham Dance Foundation since 1985, offers an insight into the making of a documentary film that is still, at the time of writing, a work in progress.

The same might be said of Cunningham's work in general. Like his long-time collaborator and companion John Cage, who died in 1992, he will no doubt remain intransigent to the last, and we honor him for it.

David Vaughan
New York October 1996

Choreography and Dance, 1997, Vol. 4(3), p. 3–15
Photocopying permitted by license only

Cunningham's Recent Work: Does It Tell a Story?

Joan Acocella

Cunningham has always insisted that the meaning of his dances consists in the movement itself, but many people have seen in his work of the 1980s a new expressionism, whether tragic or comic. This is discussed with reference to specific works from *Quartet* (1982) to *Trackers* (1991); the conclusion is that such meanings, if they are present, are nevertheless conveyed through movement alone.

KEY WORDS   Cunningham, chance, meaning, movement

One day in 1987, at a conference in New York called "Merce Cunningham and the New Dance," the conference participants were saying the usual things about Merce Cunningham: how he used chance techniques to force his imagination past conventional patterns of theatrical movement, how he separated dance from decor and music in order to avoid any overdirective unity of impression – anything that would force a "meaning" on his audience – and how, by these means, he released dance from any referential necessity, restoring to it its true, self-sufficient essence. Then, in the midst of this listing of Cunningham's exemplary achievements in the service of modernist autotelism, the great Cunningham dancer Carolyn Brown, who was one of the panelists on the stage, drew in a breath and said, "Don't believe what you're told. All those dances have stories."

This got a big laugh from the audience, a laugh that seemed to contain a measure of relief. For Brown had confirmed what many people felt they had been seeing on Cunningham's stage in the preceding years, that is, a new expressionism, a new commitment to stories and representation, to statable meaning, and above all, to tragic meaning. The work that everyone now points to in this regard is the 1982 *Quartet*, a grim piece in which four young dancers scrabbled about ignoring a fifth figure on the stage: Cunningham himself, who spent most of the dance hovering quietly in a dark corner upstage right. He was not completely ignored, however. In an unforgettable moment, one dancer, Helen Barrow, took up a position in the center of the stage, unfolded her leg in a majestic *développé* in Cunningham's direction, and then stood there on one leg for what seemed like three minutes, never looking at Cunningham but still pointing her leg in his direction. If he had seemed isolated before, this gesture isolated him further. It made him seem like a ghost, like something that was haunting her briefly, but that would eventually go away.

This is just a reading, but the title of the piece seemed to confirm that reading. For *Quartet* was not a quartet; it was a quintet. By leaving one person out of the title, Cunningham seemed to be saying that, yes, this was a piece about being left out, forgotten – a piece, even, about dying. (His quick, unceremonious exit, unnoticed by the others, shortly before the end of the piece was truly unsettling.) My knowledge of the Cunningham repertory is limited – I didn't start seeing his

Figure 1   Merce Cunningham with Karen Radford, Helen Barrow, Susan Quinn Young, and Rob Remley in *Quartet*. Photo: © 1986 JoAnn Baker, courtesy Cunningham Dance Foundation.

work until the late seventies, and he tends not to revive old pieces – but this was the first of his works that seemed to me, and to most of his audience, unequivocally tragic.

It was followed by others. *Pictures*, of 1984, is not exactly tragic, but it is full of melancholy. To David Behrman's plangent violin score, the dancers moved across the stage, going from group pose to group pose, poses which were then held and back-lit, so that the dancers become silhouettes, stilled for our contemplation. It appeared to be a dance about making dances. "These are the pictures that I make," Cunningham seemed to be saying, and in so saying, he offered himself too as an object of contemplation: the maker. Indeed, at the end of the piece, he literally showed himself as such, entering to take part in the final section and then, in the last tableau, picking up his newest dancer, Patricia Lent, and holding her stiffly across his body, as if she were a large doll. Having showed us his dance, he now showed us the clay from which it was made, a body in whose stiffness and stillness we could read, by implication, all that it means to charge a body with movement. But again, the demonstration set Cunningham apart. If we were contemplating, so was he. We saw him seeing, from a distance, and seeing himself as well as his dancers: Cunningham at Colonus.

According to the Cunningham company archivist, David Vaughan, who is writing a critical biography of the choreographer, Cunningham's tendency to present himself in his work as a thing apart from his dancers dates back at least as far as *Rebus*, of 1975. It is there too, very strikingly, in the 1978 *Exchange* and the 1981 *Gallopade*. But in *Exchange* his role, while separate, is heroic, and in *Gallopade*,

Figure 2 Merce Cunningham with Judy Lazaroff, Rob Remley, and Robert Swinston in *Gallopade*. Photo: Johan Elbers.

where it is not heroic but somewhat piteous, it is at least cushioned in comedy. By the time of *Quartet*, however, the separation has become a matter of real grief. Then in 1984 comes the contemplative mood of *Pictures*; then, in the 1987 *Fabrications*, a more elegiac view of separateness.

Fabrications is a large group piece. The women are in dresses – a costume seldom seen on Cunningham's stage – and the men in trousers and shirts, so that they look like people, not just dancers, and in a manner more frankly representational than is usual in Cunningham, they seem to portray "youth." They do what youth does, as seen by age; they dance together, they have troubles and comfort each other, they fly around, in bursts of unbounded energy. All this gives the piece a reminiscential tone, heightened by the score, Emanuel Dimas de Melo Pimenta's *Short Waves*, a scratchy, mixed business of music and static, in which old radio broadcasts surface occasionally in indistinct patches, like something heard from a distance. *Fabrications* is one of a type that I would call the aging-artist-looks-back-on-his-past ballet (cf. Antony Tudor's *The Leaves Are Fading*, Jerome Robbins' *Watermill* and *Ives, Songs*), the best of the damp-eyed genre. And in the course of the piece, the aging artist himself appears. Cunningham makes several entries, dancing first with one woman, then with another, but never actually becoming part of the group. What *Quartet* was in darkness, *Fabrications* is in sunlight. In any case, Cunningham is again a ghost.

Figure 3   Merce Cunningham with Patricia Lent, Helen Barrow, Victoria Finlayson, and Karen Radford in *Fabrications*. Photo: Jed Downhill.

The tragedy was not always about him, though, or even about aging or being an artist. The starkest portrait of anguish I ever saw on Cunningham's stage was *Shards*, made in 1987, the same year as *Fabrications*, and Cunningham did not appear in it. As the curtain rose, eight dancers dressed in grey and black stood rooted to their appointed spots on the stage. In the course of the dance, they moved into one another's space and danced together, but always returning to their original posts, as if they were imprisoned there – a sense of confinement underlined by the fact that until the very end, no one left the stage. No exit. (Nor did anyone enter, whereas in most Cunningham works people are continually going in and out.) And again in a manner more representational, more mimetic, than is usual with Cunningham, they seemed to be in the throes of some terrible anguish. They slumped their heads forward, as if in grief; they bent their heads backward, as if putting a question to God. They looked as though they were waiting for some dreaded event: a missile fired but not yet fallen, a school bus full of children lost but not yet found. In one recurring motif, a woman would stretch herself supine across a man's lap, and he would bend her shoulders and legs upward, in an aching curve. In the end, with no resolution, all the dancers simply left the stage. It was in the same month as the New York premieres of *Shards* and *Fabrications*, March 1987, that Carolyn Brown made her remark about all of Cunningham's dances having stories, and so her words seemed very timely. Whether or not his pieces had always had stories, they seemed to have stories now.

That same month, I had a brief interview with Cunningham, and I asked him: Did his dances have stories? Was there, as the reviewers were saying, a new emotionalism in his work? No, he replied. His dances had no stories, never had had stories, and if people were seeing a new emotionalism in his work, "it's just in their eyes." Or maybe it was there, he said, but "I don't put it in the piece. My choices are made in the *movement*."

Movement, he went to say, could have a strong emotional resonance. "Movement is expressive. I've never denied that. I don't think there's such a thing as abstract dance." In his dances, though, the movement was never "expressive of a particular thing."

But what about *Quartet*? What about just the title? Wasn't that expressive of a particular thing: the exclusion of the fifth character, his character? That was one possible interpretation, he said, but – and here he smiled a Mona Lisa smile – there was another possible interpretation as well. Two of the four younger dancers tended to do identical movements. So, he explained, you could count them as one. Hence "quartet."[1] No exclusion, no story.

All right, but what about *Shards*? Surely *Shards* was expressive of a particular thing, namely pain. Well, he said, maybe that one did relate to something specific, or so it had seemed to him once he looked at what he had made. "All these dismal things that are going on in the world," he said,

> the isolation and the sickness and the governments and the pollution – it's so frightful, over the whole world. Whereas we should be living in a single thing, all we have are these countries fighting each other, and what are we going to do about missiles for you and missiles for them.... And so I thought, after I began to see the material that I had made, "Well, that must be where it comes from."

But he didn't consciously put it here. In explaining this to me, he went so far as to claim that even his structural methods – his breaking up of conventional dramatic logic, his avoidance of development and climax – were also a sort of reflection of the way of the world: "I think the whole society's broken up that way. How many climaxes can you have each day? One from China and one from Peru and fifteen from over there?"

What he appeared to be saying – and it is a position consistent with his longtime interest in Zen – was that if, in his work, he represented things, he did so passively. These things flowed through him, into the work, while he simply concentrated on the movement. (One is reminded of Stravinsky's statement that he was merely the "vessel" for *Le Sacre du Printemps*. To see this echt-romantic idea expressed by these echt-modernist artists is something of a lesson.) There was also the suggestion, as in Zen, that it was this very posture of humility, of not having a meaning to impose, that permitted him to transmit meanings truer than he could manufacture. By avoiding meaning – by cutting the threads of dramatic logic and scrambling the pieces – he put himself in a position to reveal the true logic of the cosmos, normally obscured by our meaning-hungry minds. I asked him what he thought of this idea. "Perhaps," he said.

Since that year, 1987, Cunningham's work has shown a marked retrenchment from its former tragic mood. I wonder if this reversal, however natural, might not have been hastened by the press. In many of the discussions of Cunningham's "new emotionalism" there was a certain note of smugness. "Aha!" the reviewers

---

[1]   This interpretation of the title was also proposed by David Vaughan in "New York Dance/Merce Cunningham," *Financial Times* (London), 12 April 1983.

aying. "Now we've got him. For thirty years he's driven us crazy, dances that we couldn't understand. Now at last he's found out he's ...n, learned to tell a story." Such reviews cannot have been pleasing to him. And I was certainly not the only journalist who came to him and pressed him on the subject of his emotions. For the famously private Cunningham, this was probably very irritating.

Whatever the reasons, the two new works presented in Cunningham's next New York season, 1988, were notably emotionless. One of them, *Eleven*, had eleven dancers (no more misnumberings) dressed in inexplicably paint-smeared clothes and performing in front of a brick wall. Accompanying them was an excerpt from Robert Ashley's *Odalisque*, a witty chant-dialogue in which the captain and lieutenant of a flying saucer have an absurd discussion about an American musician they have taken on board. Here again was the old Cunninghamesque cleavage of dance, decor, and music. The dance had no more apparent relation to the score than the score to the decor, beyond the fact that all of them were in some measure elusive. The same was true of the second piece, *Carousal*. The dancers wore bizarre costumes and manipulated a large, snaky rope. The dance had some comic elements and some sinister elements, but these never came together into a comprehensible whole. So much for the new emotionalism. What we seemed to be seeing here was the very opposite of emotionalism – something closer to what was said to be Cunningham's old, cool style of the sixties.

Curiously, one of the most emotional-looking works of that season was from those cool sixties: *RainForest* (1968), with its famous set – a flock of silver pillows – by Andy Warhol. Asked by the *New York Times* why he had chosen to revive *RainForest* at this time, Cunningham said he figured he had probably done it as a tribute to Warhol. (Warhol had just died.) It is also possible, though, that he was trying to make a point. In answering questions about the "new emotionalism," he had always insisted that if people saw emotion in his work, this was nothing new. His dances, he said, had always been emotional (or expressive, to use his word), and films of certain of his early dances, such as the very heated *Crises* of 1960, prove his point. But these are archival films. Here in the *RainForest* revival was the living proof. Despite Warhol's silver pillows and David Tudor's chirping score, the piece was truly scarifying. The dancers scuttled across the floor on their stomachs. They pitched themselves at one another, hung from one another, attached themselves to one another like growths. You couldn't call this a story. Still, the dance had a definite and unified emotional thrust: horror without pathos.

So there it was – old work of extreme "expressiveness," new work of extreme coolness and elusiveness. Q.E.D. The season could have been entitled "There Is No New Emotionalism in My Work."

Since that 1988 season Cunningham's output has included some very somber works. *Cargo X* of 1989 looked a little like a religious ceremony, perhaps a mass for the dead. There was a ladder at the back of the stage that the dancers kept decorating with flowers, like an altar. The music, by Takehisa Kosugi, had a wailing note. (Kosugi played a tape of a flamenco singer and sang along with it.) The dance too had an impassioned, even angry character. At the opening David Kulick charged forward, lifting his fists in the air, leaping and leaping in *passé*; other solos were equally ferocious.

Darker still was *Polarity* of 1990. Again and again in this piece two or three dancers would come together, stand still, and then slowly rotate their hands or their feet,

Figure 4   Alan Good and Patricia Lent in *Polarity*. Photo: Jed Downhill.

as if they were speaking to one another in some kind of a code language, telling a secret, and not a nice one. Another keynote of the piece was support – one person holding up another – and as the dance progressed, the support became more and more extreme, the supported person more and more helpless. As always in Cunningham's work, there were sudden dynamic shifts, changes from fast to slow and back, but here things seemed to get slower and slower. Something dire was happening, you felt. At the end, in the most extreme image of support, a woman (Kimberly Bartosik) was hoisted, supine, over the shoulder of a man and pinned there in the air, arching backwards, thrashing her legs slowly. She seemed to be dying.

But neither *Cargo X* nor *Polarity* had the real knife-thrust of *Quartet* or even *Fabrications*. Both were more enigmatic than tragic, a fact that was due partly to their decors. *Cargo X*'s flower-decked ladder had as much of a daffy, flower-power look as an ecclesiastical character. As for *Polarity*, its backdrop was an enlargement of two nature drawings by Cunningham – one of a jackrabbit, one of an owl and another bird – and these plain creatures of the earth, inexpertly drawn, softened the menace of the piece. In both *Cargo X* and *Polarity* it seemed as though passionate feelings had been reassimilated into an attitude of objectivity. Indeed, one felt this already in *Points in Space*, which was first performed live in 1987, the same year as *Shards* and *Fabrications*.[2] *Points in Space* featured a long, slow male-female duet of huge intensity, but like the comparable duet in *Channels/Inserts* from 1981 (before the "new emotionalism"), it was repeatedly interrupted, and its intensity thus repeatedly challenged. This was the old Cunningham dance-as-time-space-phenomenon: lots of things happening at once, and nothing the boss.

As I said, *Polarity* was backed by Cunningham's nature drawings. He has done many such drawings. (There was a whole show of his animal drawings at the Margarete Roeder Gallery in early 1990.) He loves nature, and that love has gone into his work, not just in obvious instances like *Inlets* and *Inlets 2*, where the dancers move like fish, but in more general ways. The very objectivity of Cunningham's world – the seeming randomness, the lack of hierarchy, the simultaneity of events, the sheer busy-ness, with all those entrances and exits – looks like nature. And after the "new emotionalism" and what appears to have been his recoil from it in early 1988, the next work that Cunningham created was a poem to nature: *Five Stone Wind*.

When *Five Stone Wind* had its premiere at the 1988 Avignon Festival, it was performed outdoors. By the time of its New York premiere, it had moved indoors, but it still looked like an outdoor piece. The colored ropes that Mark Lancaster, the set designer, hung from the flies to the stage seemed to connect the earth and the sky. The title, of course, with its stone and wind, also pointed to nature. And when Cunningham entered, his first action was to gaze upward and open his arms to the sky. "Behold the world," he seemed to say.

The rest of the dance was a measured progress toward this ecstatic conclusion. After a slow opening section, the dancers onstage were repeatedly interrupted by three small women who raced through in tiny, quick steps and then flew into the wings. These women were the wind, Cunningham told a journalist. In the second half of the dance, the wind women flew through again and again, and the other

---

[2]   A video version came out in 1986.

dancers began slowly joining their ranks. This was accomplished at first by costume changes. Originally, only the wind women were in leotards. The other women
were in skirts, the men in trousers. Gradually, however, the non-wind women,
during their exits, changed into trousers. Gender was thus eliminated, and with
it some measure of individuality. Then all the dancers, men and women, began
returning from their exits in unitards or leotards, just like the wind women. They
all became wind. And soon they took on the wind-women's movements. By the
end, they were all leaping and flying. What had started out human and male-
female and individualized had now resolved itself into a general image: pure
cosmos.

August Pace (1989), which was produced the year after *Five Stone Wind*, was
probably also about nature, though on the surface it was about something else:
world peace. Created amid the euphoria accompanying Mikhail Gorbachev's early
reforms in the Soviet Union, *August Pace* was America's first *glasnost* ballet. It had
a set by the young Soviet painter Afrika (Sergei Bugaev) – the first Soviet-Ameri-
can dance collaboration in many a decade – and a thrillingly propulsive score by
Michael Pugliese that combined instruments from all over the world: Chinese
tomtoms, Tibetan finger cymbals, a Brazilian berimbau, and so forth. Aptly, the
score was entitled *Peace Talks*. The dancing too seemed to speak of reconciliation:
the piece was mostly duets, and in most of the duets one person would repeatedly
go off balance – tilt, lurch, fall – and have to be righted by the other. It was thus
a dance of strenuous cooperation and, as such, a potent and unsentimental hymn
to world peace.

At the same time, though, as a kind of outer rim on its peace message, *August
Pace* was again a hymn to nature, to the world of innocent life that war endangers,
peace preserves. More than other Cunningham dances, it seemed full of animal
imagery: storky leg-liftings, horsey prances, rabbity hops. At one point, Larissa
McGoldrick, one of the troupe's younger dancers, came onstage and lifted her big,
beautiful leg first behind her, then to the side, then to the front, but all in a completely unassuming manner, like a bird unfolding its wings between alighting and
takeoff. This matter-of-factness extended to the dance as a whole. Grave things
happened in it – at one point three people bent over a body that looked to be dead
– but other things didn't stop happening as a result. Just as in nature, life went on.

It is possible to view these two clear-headed, happy dances as a sweeping of the
decks. After them, in any case, Cunningham returned to a kind of norm. His two
new works of 1991, though they had none of the euphoria of *Five Stone Wind* and
August Pace – indeed, their emotional life was thorny, enigmatic, in the usual
Cunningham manner – were nevertheless markedly objective. *Neighbors*, the
first of the 1991 works, had a dolls-come-to-life theme. The backdrop, by Mark
Lancaster, was a composition of Harlequinesque triangles; the costumes, also by
Lancaster, looked like deluxe doll outfits; and the dancers did doll-like things.
They rotated their joints, jumped like jesters, flopped over from the waist. The
interest of the dance lay in the tension between this quaint, corny theme and the
amount of sheer strangeness that accumulated in the piece. At one point a doll
seemed to expire, or at least wind down. At other points the dolls appeared to be
using *petits battements* to send Morse-code messages to one another. The dance
seemed to be exploring a world where psychology is completely a function of
movement, of the movement mechanism. What all this meant to a 72-year-old
dancer/choreographer whose own movement mechanism was failing him can be

Figure 5 Larissa McGoldrick, Victoria Finlayson, Alan Good, and Robert Swinston in *Neighbors*. Photo: Jed Downhill.

speculated on. (In this season, for the first time, Cunningham had to begin casting other dancers even in his late, "old-man" roles; Alan Good took his great role in *Exchange*.) But the point is that such meaning as the piece had was wholly absorbed by the movement. There was no story that lay outside dancing.

This was all the more true of *Trackers*. In this piece Cunningham pushed his quest for objectivity to what would appear to be its outer limit: he choreographed the dance on a computer, using a new computer program, called LifeForms, that had recently been developed (with his help) at Simon Fraser University to aid in the choreographic process. At a press conference preceding *Trackers'* premiere, Cunningham showed how LifeForms worked. For every detail of the dance, down to wrist rotations, the computer offered a "menu" of multiple possibilities to choose from. If ever Cunningham had sought a way to free his mind from cliché, to bypass the accustomed itineraries of theatrical movement (mimetic gesture, spatial hierarchy, development and climax, beginning-middle-and-end), this was it, for the machine had no sentimental preferences for one movement over another. And if *Trackers* had a fault, it was that the piece was so unsentimental, that it seemed not to be a piece at all. It was a real test-tube baby.

One aspect of it was very interesting, though, and that was Cunningham's own role. Again he portrayed himself as separate from the other dancers, but here the separation was truly drastic. Whereas the others moved about freely, he danced

Figure 6 Merce Cunningham with Michael Cole, Emily Navar, and Robert Wood in *Trackers*. Photo: Johan Elbers.

with the support of a portable barre that he brought onstage with him. As the dance progressed and the dancers moved, en masse, to the right or the left, he would hurriedly move the barre so as to remain part of their grouping. This image of Merce Cunningham hauling support equipment around in order to keep up with his dancers was unsettling – the more so in that the metal barre, as he moved it, came to look like a walker – but it was also funny, a nice bit of black comedy. Whatever his grief about the end of his dancing career, in this piece it had been reabsorbed into comedy, reobjectified – accepted, as it were. If so, the wealth of complication in the other dancers' steps, full of LifeForms-derived ingenuities, may have been an additional comment on this difficult situation. "Perhaps I can't dance," Cunningham might have been saying, "but I can certainly make dances." Actually, the same message could be read at the end of *Five Stone Wind*. In the final tableau the other dancers stood with their feet apart, Cunningham with his feet together. "They will dance, I won't," he seemed to say, and the mood was one of acceptance.

This matter of the ability to dance is key to Cunningham's works, and not just the works that brood on his loss of that ability. Indeed, if *Five Stone Wind* is about nature, the aspect of nature that it most forthrightly celebrates is the capacity to move. The title of the piece alludes to movement – the "five," as a company press release explained, were the five points on the stage at which the dancers entered and exited – and in no other recent work of Cunningham's do the dancers move as exuberantly as in this one. (By the end, as I said, they were all flying.) At one point in the piece he gives an actual lesson in movement. One of the women (Kristy Santimyer at the New York premiere) goes up to him, and he takes her arm in one hand and her leg in the other and begins tipping her back and forth in a seesawing arabesque. "Look!" he seems to be saying. "Look at what these dancers can do. They can bend this way and that. They can move in this direction and that direction." And as he shows us all the ways she can go, Santimyer is suddenly no longer a woman or even a dancer but a sort of concatenation of *directions*. Arcs and spirals, circle and lines, form in the air around her: all her movement possibilities. Oskar Schlemmer, the Bauhaus artist, made dance pieces like this – mystical visions about sheer kinetic possibility. In *Five Stone Wind* Cunningham seemed to be gazing at the same vision.

To say that a dance is about dancing is very unsatisfying to many people; it seems too reflexive, too hieratic – ungiving. Hence the note of celebration in the discussions of Cunningham's "new emotionalism" of the early eighties. But even in the works of the "new emotionalism" the most potent images were not mimetic images – that is, images based on the gestural drama of everyday life – but dance images. After all, the thing that bespoke Cunningham's isolation in *Quartet* and *Fabrications* was the simple fact that he was not dancing with the others. Even in its smallest details, his plight in these dances was a dance plight. He did not hide his face in his hands or raise his fists to heaven. He danced with his arms – that is, the two limbs that he could still move easily. Even in those movements that seemed mimetic, the eloquence was less gestural than sheerly kinetic. When he made his terrible exit as the end of *Quartet*, it was not so much the exit that was unsettling as its attack, or lack of attack. Like a person who has waited in line at the post office for too long, he just walked out. He gave up.

In these works, then, dance is not simply the medium; it is the story. If there was a new emotionalism in Cunningham's work of the early eighties, the tragedy that unleashed those emotions was not old age or the thought of death but the fact of not being able to dance. When, in the works of that period, he shows himself prevented from dancing, this is not a metaphor. It is the problem. For him, this was death enough.

And for him dancing is meaning enough. No great choreographer has ever been more avoidant of literary meaning than Cunningham, and in his lesser works we can see the danger of that avoidance: dryness. In his anxiety to remain a virgin, he becomes a spinster. But in his stronger works – the majority of his works – the dancing, despite the lack of reference to "life," does add up to a reflection on life. It is, to begin with, a celebration of energy. Cunningham is a vitalist. In the interview I had with him in 1987, when he denied that he gave his work any meaning, he added, "I'm not out to confuse, but I really have insisted always – it has been my life – that dancing has its own life. It does not need something else. It can have other things. Obviously it can. But what makes it alive is the dancing."

He has had his way. His dancing looks supremely alive, partly because it carries no heavy cargo of meaning. But it is not devoid of meaning or isolated from meaning; it is pre-meaning. In its combination of concentration with things that would seem to threaten concentration (busy-ness, interruption, energy shifts), it is the image of the mind at work before it reaches conclusions. In other words, it is the image of intelligence. And that is the sense one gets every spring in New York when the curtain goes up on the Cunningham season: suddenly everything seems smart, vital, fresh. As for meanings, they are there, but *in statu nascendi*. What Cunningham wants to give us is not the flower – leave that to others – but the stem.

Choreography and Dance, 1997, Vol. 4(3), p. 17–28
Photocopying permitted by license only

Merce Cunningham and Meaning: The Zen Connection

Marilyn Vaughan Drown

Over the years, Merce Cunningham has confounded the efforts of dance historians and theoreticians who attempt to classify and define his work. Because of the innovative nature of his choreography, some wrongly assume the dances have no meaning beyond fleeting impressions derived from the collage-like effect of visual and aural stimuli. This paper takes the position that the dances do, in fact, have profound meaning, based on a comparison between Cunningham's aesthetic and the attitude toward meaning found in the Zen Arts.

Cunningham's use of chance procedures in his choreographic process, and his independent collaborations with other artists in the design and musical accompaniment, are essential elements of his work which emphasize the spiritual as opposed to the personal in his art. By showing the many similarities between the Zen aesthetic and Cunningham's, this paper demonstrates the metaphysical meaning of his work – meaning resplendent with significance and profundity.

KEY WORDS   Cunningham, Meaning, Zen

> *The mountain air sparkles as the sun sets,*
> *Birds in flocks return together.*
> *In these things there is fundamental truth,*
> *But when I start to explain it, I lose the words.*

T'ao Ch'ien (326–397)[1]

Merce Cunningham has a body of work which consists of over one hundred pieces of choreography and he continues to create new works for stage and video. His tremendous contribution to contemporary art involves not only his ongoing influence in the world of dance, but in the other arts as well – as innovator and collaborator. The innovative nature of Cunningham's work, however, confounds the efforts of dance historians and theoreticians who try to classify and define such things as genre, style, interpretation of meaning, and philosophic import. Described variously as modernist, post-modernist, and neo-classicist, Cunningham has employed divergent styles that range from the virtuosity of ballet technique to the minimalism of pedestrian movement. By continually experimenting with artistic possibilities, which free his dances from predictability, he eliminates many of the familiar references used to decipher meaning and intention in choreographic art. Consequently, some viewers wrongly assume the dances have no meaning

---

[1]   See Stephen Addiss (1989), p. 166.

beyond fleeting impressions derived from the collage-like effect of visual and aural stimuli. Some feel he is a clever manipulator, trying to confuse his audience. Some see him as a consummate purist, interested only in movement for its own sake. However, others have found a way of interpreting the works of Cunningham which suggests there is meaning both rich in its complexity and profound in its implications – an interpretive approach closely related to the attitude towards meaning found in the Zen arts. This paper discusses the nature of meaning as it applies to Cunningham's work, then analyzes the way the Zen aesthetic gives insight into the meaning of Cunningham's work.

According to the philosopher Francis Sparshott (1985), "Most discussions of dance meaning in the context of aesthetics fasten on specific meanings of specific movements." In order to develop a "general theory of dance," he states, "one has therefore to determine the scope of the meaningfulness of dance." Starting with the consideration that "the very fact of dance has meaning," he goes on to differentiate between the meaning derived from the experience of the dance and from reflections made about dance, as well as the distinction between meaning for the observer and meaning for the dancer. He also lists four "essential elements" which consist of music, place, and costume, as well as the significance of "being a dancer" (ibid.).

Sparshott's method of determining the dimensions of meaning for dance in general is an appropriate starting point for the consideration of meaning in the dances of Cunningham as well. For Cunningham, being a dancer and making dances are significant activities in themselves with inherent potential for evoking meaningful experiences for the dancers and the viewers. The basic material of dance is movement and the basic nature of movement, as Cunningham (1985) states, "is expressive, regardless of intentions of expressivity, beyond intention." The expressive qualities of movement are not manipulated by Cunningham in the usual manner, however, and meaning in relation to the expressive nature of the movement must be considered in the context of the structural and theatrical devices he employs.

The choices Cunningham makes regarding the way his dances are choreographed and the way they are presented become important aspects of meaning. These are the essential elements of his dances which lead to a particular kind of experience for the dancer, the viewers, or the theorist who, upon reflection, attempts to interpret the experience in an appropriate manner. The use of chance procedures[2] as a means of composition is one of the essential elements of Cunningham's work. Chance procedures involve randomly selecting by various means the elements of each dance. Another related essential element is Cunningham's approach to working with artists, designers, and composers – most notably, John Cage. Working together for over fifty years, they created the dance and the music independently from one another. According to their method of collaboration, the dancers do not hear the score until after the dance is

---

[2] As one example, Cunningham often uses the method of tossing coins for the determination of chance procedures. [To consult *The I Ching* one must either throw yarrow sticks or toss coins to determine the outcome.] For a thorough explanation of Cunningham's use of chance see Carolyn Brown's (1968) article, "On Chance" in *Ballet Review* 2:2, pp. 7–24.

choreographed and rehearsed. Often the score itself is produced through chance procedures as it is being performed. The dancers do not dance to the music, they dance to counts Cunningham devises based on a prepared time structure. The music and dance co-exist in time and share a common frame based on the determined length of the piece being performed.

Along with the musical accompaniment, the stage design and costumes are also created independently – any of these may also be devised through chance procedures. Therefore, the theatrical elements combine with the structural elements of the dances in unpredictable ways, both simultaneously and sequentially. Even though Cunningham's performances are put together in unusual ways, in many of his dances the collaborations between the various artists are not totally arbitrary. They often reveal loosely formed connections to a particular fact that Cunningham shares about the dance he is creating. Consequently, Cunningham's pieces demonstrate a kind of cohesion, in spite of the independent collaborations and non-linear nature of the work.

For the dance *Summerspace*, choreographed in 1958, Cunningham (1985) recalls relating to Robert Rauschenberg. "One thing I can tell you about this dance is it has no center." Rauschenberg's design, which consists of pointillist costumes and matching backdrop, creates the shimmering sensation that the space itself is visible. The non-metric, atmospheric quality of the musical accompaniment, by Morton Feldman, further enhances the impression that the space is as palpable as the bodies that dart, whirl, fly, float, and careen through it. The multi-directional movement and focus allow the dancers to explore and define space, not just occupy it. Instead of offering spatial arrangements created to present dancing to an audience, Cunningham uses dynamic relationships to transform the stage into an energized force field. The viewer's focus continually shifts as the dancers create a state of flux. The stage is so fully utilized both horizontally and vertically that the dance spills over into the wings and out towards the audience, obliterating the usual relationship between center stage and the important action of a dance. The dance conveys a powerful sense of the exhilaration continuous movement offers – transforming the various essential elements into a meaningful experience for the viewer.

Cunningham relies on the viewer to assimilate the various elements of each work. He has often stated that interpretations should be based on personal responses to a particular dance. Some viewers, however, are confounded by the multiplicity in Cunningham's dances and are unable to understand the innovative nature of the work. Dance critic Jack Anderson (1975–76) recognizes this interpretive dilemma when he writes: "Merce Cunningham has often been a problem. His treatment of music and decor has been a problem. His utilization of chance has been a problem. The latest problem Cunningham has posed for dancegoers is that of the Theater Event." Nevertheless, Anderson goes on to offer an insightful interpretation of "Events"[3] that applies appropriately to all of Cunningham's choreography:

---

[3]   Since 1964, Cunningham has performed over five hundred Events, combining dances in different ways to adapt to particular performance needs and available space.

Figure 1   Viola Farber and Carolyn Brown in *Summerspace*. Photo: Richard Rutledge.

There is, though, at least one way of regarding Events which can make them less forbidding, a point of view emanating from the philosophy which produced them in the first place. Cunningham, John Cage, and other artists in their circle regard art as an imitation of nature – but not in any literal sense, for that might result in nothing more than a superfluous replication of objects. Rather, they wish to imitate nature in its manner of operation. For them, the universe is Heraclitean, forever open to metamorphosis. Events, then, are attempts to reproduce in miniature the workings of the universe.... The 'experience of the dance' Cunningham says he desires Events to provide is thus very much like the experience of life itself.

How do Cunningham's dances create a sense of "life itself" as Anderson suggests? The reasons involve the diversity and complexity of the essential elements of his work, as mentioned above, as well as the way these activities imitate nature in its manner of operation. The philosophy behind such an aesthetic is found in the Zen attitude toward the spiritual connection between life and art. Zen teacher Daisetz Suzuki (1970) writes: "... the relationship rises from an appreciation of the significance of life – or we may say the mysteries of life enter deeply into the composition of art. When an art, therefore, presents those mysteries in a profound and creative manner, it moves us to the depths of our being; art then becomes a divine work." Regardless of the specific content or subject matter of a piece, the substance of Cunningham's work seems to deal with the "mysteries of life" that Suzuki discusses.

Cunningham's attitude about the use of chance procedures as a choreographic tool reveals the spiritual dimension in his work. He (1955) writes, "... the feeling I have when I compose in this way is that I am in touch with natural resources far greater than my own personal inventiveness could ever be, much more universally human than the particular habits of my own practice, and organically rising out of common pools of motor impulses."

Zen artists offer aesthetic experiences based on similar attitudes about process and creativity. The metaphysical nature of these experiences indicates a viewpoint that is very different from the Western tradition that separates secular and religious art. Philosopher Alan Watts (1957) states:

> ... the art forms which Zen has created are not symbolic in the same way as other types of Buddhist art, or as is 'religious' art as a whole. The favorite subjects of Zen artists ... are what we should call natural, concrete, and secular things.... Furthermore, the arts of Zen are not merely or primarily representational.... Even in painting, the work of art is considered not only as representing nature but as being itself a work of nature. For the very technique involves the art of artlessness, or what Sabro Hasegawa has called the 'controlled accident'....

In Zen aesthetics there is "no conflict between the natural element of chance and the human element of control" (ibid.). This observation is also true of Cunningham's work.

The idea of the "controlled accident" applies appropriately to Cunningham's chance procedures, as well as his method of working with artistic collaborators. Cage (1968) describes the collaborative nature of their work in these terms: "The two arts (music and dance) take place in a common place and time, but each art expresses this Space-Time in its own way. The result is an activity of interpenetrations in time and space, not counterpoints, nor controlled relationships, but flexibilities as are known from the mobiles of Alexander Calder." An example of this can be found in Cage's work *Voiceless Essay* which accompanies *Points in Space*, choreographed in 1986. A collage of whispering voices sometimes accentuates movement and sometimes stillness – either of which becomes appropriate without being predictable.

Another connection between Zen and Cunningham's aesthetic is evident in the analogy he makes between his view of movement and the *koan*[4] defining the term as "two things going on, so that you are in a sense ready to go, but in a sense going all the time" (Cunningham, 1985). An interesting parallel could be drawn between the core of this analogy and Zen *haiku*, "... tiny seventeen-syllable poems that seek to convey a sudden awareness of beauty by a mating of opposite or incongruous terms. Thus the classical *haiku* characteristically fuses motion and stillness" (Seidensticker, 1960). Indeed, a signature of Cunningham choreography is stillness juxtaposed with movement in a way that illuminates the essence of both. In the dance *Pictures*, choreographed in 1984, dancers suspend movement in a way that creates the sensation they are vibrating with energy. The dancers never look as if they are posing, even when they hold difficult positions like standing on one leg for long periods of time. Cunningham (1985) explains how he avoids a "static quality" in moments of stillness on stage: "Even when we are still we are moving, we are not waiting for something, we are in action when we are still."

Like Cunningham's dances, Zen *haiku* are non-linear in both content and form. They are non-narrative, creating what Watts (1957) describes as "word-less poetry." He explains: "... a good haiku is a pebble thrown into the pool of the listener's mind, evoking associations out of the richness of his own memory. It invites the listener to participate...." The poem by the Zen monk Ryokan: *"The sound of the scouring/Of the saucepan blends/With the tree-frogs' voices"* juxtaposes seemingly unrelated events in a way similar to juxtapositions between the movements, music, and design in Cunningham's dances. This celebration of multiplicity seems to expand time and space, with the potential for expanding consciousness as well.

In the Zen arts, Stephen Addiss (1989) explains, there is always an attempt to "[eliminate] nonessential elements." He continues: "In this way the viewer can focus his or her attention upon such Zen principles as unity of subject and object, concentration of spirit, and avoidance of overt emotional displays." Likewise, for Cunningham the personality of the dancer, as well as the choreographer, is submerged, creating the sense of *being the art* as well as the artist. Cunningham (1955) describes this stage of concentration: "[as] tranquility ... which allows the dancer to detach himself and thereby to present freely and liberally. Making himself such a kind of nature puppet that he is as if dancing on a string which is like an umbilical cord: mother-nature and father-spirit moving his limbs, without thought." In Cunningham's dances each dancer remains an individual yet transcends the tendency to telegraph emotional contexts through the usual kinds of dramatic gestures and theatrical dynamics. The performance quality that emerges is one of intense commitment to the movement itself. Carolyn Brown, principal dancer for the Cunningham Dance Company from its inception in 1953 until 1972, embodied this unique movement style. In the film of *Walkaround Time*, choreographed in 1968, she combines fluidity with control, demonstrating amazing virtuosity in her balance and concentration. A meditative quality permeates her face and movements, bringing to mind the tranquility found in the Zen arts, as well as Cunningham's passage quoted above.

---

[4]   Koans are Zen riddles designed to inspire paradoxical thinking. In transcending logical or linear thinking patterns, one is able to embrace opposites and gain enlightenment.

Cunningham's choreography encompasses other important aspects of the Zen arts. Author Nancy Wilson Ross (1966) discusses two elements of Zen aesthetics which apply to Cunningham as well. One is that the artist "should be free of all thought of himself" as well as any ideas of intention that could limit the artistic possibilities. The other is that his "concern should be ... to capture a moment in a process, one stage in an invisible chain of growth." Cunningham avoids ego-related concerns as a means of artistic expression, choosing instead opportunities for spontaneity and expansion.

Taoism, an ancient Chinese philosophy reflected in *The I Ching: Or Book of Changes* (Wilhem & Baynes, 1967), and a precursor of Zen, depicts the basic principle of life as transformation. In Cunningham's dances the emphasis is also on transformation. This image of change is created by the lack of a specific focal point and the way groupings unpredictably change into different formations. The stage space fluctuates, expanding and contracting along with the viewer's sense of time. In the dance *Points in Space*, the dancers create a kaleidoscopic effect by creating peripheral movements that catch the eye, only to change into new formations that, again, transform into something else. These changing patterns, groupings of dancers which are at one point asymmetrical and complex in arrangement, then symmetrical and simple, lead to the sensation that the space/time continuum can be made visible in relation to the human activities that take place on the stage.

In Cunningham's video projects he deals with aspects of movement in relation

Figure 2   L–R Robert Swinston, Catherine Kerr, Judy Lazaroff, Rob Remley, Susan Emery, and Megan Walker in *Channels/Inserts*. Photo: Johan Elbers.

to time and space in ways that are particularly effective within that medium. In *Channels/Inserts*, produced in 1981, he uses different kinds of space that evoke specific images. At first the dancers are in a void-like space, large and black, which envelops them. In this space the movements are usually either slow and control-led or expansive and far-ranging. At one point the dancers create a vortex of movement within the void by leaping in large figure-eight patterns. The camera then pans back – taking into view a narrow, brightly lit space where two small figures are seen in the distance. Suddenly, in close-up, dancers fly into this smaller space, working in tight, fast movements – side to side and up and back – almost in place. This space turns out to be the hallway between the cavernous stage space seen earlier and a studio which can be seen in the mirror through its open door, reflecting the movement of the dancers working within. At one point, the dancers appear and disappear from view, then the camera follows a couple into a corner. In the next frame, three couples are standing still along the hallway and the only movement that can be seen is in the mirror of the studio – the reflection of a couple dancing. All these changes of viewpoint can be seen as transformations that occur in the life of a dancer: person to dancer, dancer to student, student to performer.

In Cunningham's work the dynamic aspect of transformation is a potent source for imagery concerning the interrelationship between human and natural events. The dances create a dynamic vision of reality, not only metaphorically, but in the actuality of human bodies moving in the context of complex spatial and temporal relationships. According to the physicist Fritjof Capra (1975), who writes about the parallels between modern physics and eastern philosophy: "The whole universe is thus engaged in endless motion and activity; in a continual cosmic dance of energy." If this image of a "cosmic dance" were to be actualized artistically, what better examples could one find than Cunningham's work? *Torse*, choreographed in 1976, contains such complexity and energy that dance critic Arlene Croce (1980) calls it the "ultimate *I Ching* ballet."[5] She continues, "The steps are utterly unforeseen permutations of academic combinations, and they come in such thick clusters that the audience is as winded as the dancers." Cunningham (1985) suggests an interpretation of meaning for the dance by offering this description: "What it amounted to was a *continual change*." The metaphor of the "cosmic dance" revealed here demonstrates the potential for meaning in Cunningham's work, illuminating the way his dances do, in fact, "imitate nature in its manner of operation."

In her book on Zen, Ross (1966) describes "certain characteristics of Zen arts such as simplicity, seeming artlessness, inwardness, emptiness, suggestibility [and] deliberate incompleteness." These qualities apply to Cunningham's dances as well; particularly, the "Event" format which Cunningham frequently uses. The video *Event for Television*, produced in 1976, displays the kind of fluid incompleteness found in the Zen arts. While each of the eight sections of the Event has its own costumes and design, the sections are not treated as separate dances. Rather, some of the sections are abruptly replaced, while others merge gradually into the next.

---

[5] Cunningham (1985) created *Torse* through a complex application of chance procedures. He explains that he used "sixty-four phrases, because that's the number of hexagrams in *The I Ching*," p. 19.

At the end of *Antic Meet*, while Cunningham – who is unsuccessfully attempting to put on a four-armed sweater that has become stuck over his head – begins tying the two extra arms into a knot, one of the Frank Stella canvas backdrops comes into view, and *Scramble* begins. Later, a dancer exiting from the *Scramble* section bumps into one of the pillows from *RainForest*, which then begins. Within dances, abrupt changes are juxtaposed with gradual metamorphosis. In *Septet*, at the end of the section, three couples are posed in different yet connected positions. A couple unrelated to the group dances behind them, then joins the group – setting off a chain reaction with each couple affecting the consequent movement of the next couple.

Irrational and humorous elements of humanity and images taken from nature, popular themes in the Zen arts, can be found in *Event for Television* as well. In *Antic Meet*, Cunningham loses the battle with the absurd sweater in comic fashion and in *Solo*, Cunningham darts out his tongue like a lizard and paws at himself like a cat. In *RainForest*, the dancers jaxtapose quick travelling movements that slice through the space with slow languid movements that involve crawling and rolling on the floor. These moments evoke visual images of the different kinds of movement found in a rain forest: perhaps the flight of a bird rapidly changing direction versus the slow steady path of the snail along the forest floor.

Figure 3 Merce Cunningham (foreground) with Barbara Dilley, Viola Farber, Shareen Blair, and Carolyn Brown in *Antic Meet*. Photo: Fannie Helen Melcer.

In the last two sections, *Westbeth* and *Video Triangle*, groups of dancers relate to each other through sharing weight and holding hands, then breaking off from the group to perform solos. Equal emphasis on each movement gives the impression that no one movement is more important than another. Yet every movement makes a unique statement, a suchness, as expressed in Zen terminology. Each dancer appears variously as soloist, partner or part of a larger group; maintaining an individuality while contributing to the "exemplification of energies" (Cunningham, 1976) achieved by the company as a whole unit.

Roger Copeland (1983), in his article "Merce Cunningham and the Politics of Perception," sees the fragmentary aspects of Cunningham's work as a "rejection of wholeness" and the movements as "devoid of expressive or symbolic elements." He attempts to prove that Cunningham intends to "root the natural out of his dancing" (ibid.). This paper contends, conversely, that the dances indicate a view of nature that is ultimately unifying and spiritual.

As the process of nature is forever in flux, so is the human being forever assimilating the changes that occur. The chance operations Cunningham employs to create dances offer the viewer surprising and illuminating juxtapositions. Nevertheless, form and content in Cunningham's dances exemplify the interconnectedness of time and space, movement and stillness, order and disorder – revealing the way these relational elements interact in art as well as in nature. Sumio Kam'bayashi (1966) describes the way opposites are expressed by explaining: "In Japan, the structural logic in art is not constructive but additive. There is not so much causal consequence as intuitive sequence. Oriental logic of BOTH/AND just juxtaposes things as they come. It is a feminine, receptive logic that rejects nothing and embraces all." He sees Cunningham's dances as an expression of this "pluralism" as he terms it: "[making] anything, even the most incongruous elements, co-exist."

Alan Watts (1957) could be discussing Cunningham's use of space in *Points in Space* when he discusses the work of the Zen artist, My-yuan: "The secret lies in knowing how to balance form with emptiness and, above all, in knowing when one has 'said' enough. For Zen spoils neither the aesthetic shock nor the satori[6] shock by filling in, by explanation, second thoughts, and intellectual commentary. Furthermore, the figure so integrally related to its empty space gives the feeling of the 'Marvelous Void' from which the event suddenly appears." The aesthetic choices made by Zen artists and Cunningham indicate a similar potential for spiritual meaning in their artistic endeavors.

In the article mentioned above, Copeland calls Cunningham's work "*perceptual training,*" recognizing a "*moral* dimension" of meaning. However, he negates the possibility of a spiritual dimension when stating: "Cunningham was the first choreographer to fully secularize the dance...." A more accurate description of Cunningham's work is perceptual liberation – indicating the way in which the viewer is allowed to get in touch with what Watts (1957) calls the "... 'original mind' which deals with life in its totality and so can do ever so many 'things' at once." Watt explains:

---

[6]   Satori is the Zen term for the experience of enlightenment.

Figure 4   Chris Komar, Robert Swinston, and Karen Radford in *Points in Space*. Photo: Robert Hill for BBC.

In its own way, each one of the arts which Zen has inspired gives vivid expression to the sudden or instantaneous quality of its view of the world. The momentariness of...*haiku*...bring[s] out the real reason why Zen has always called itself the way of instantaneous awakening. It is not just that satori comes quickly and unexpectedly, all of a sudden, for mere speed has nothing to do with it. The reason is that Zen is a liberation from time. For if we open our eyes and see clearly, it becomes obvious that there is no other time than this instant, and that the past and the future are abstractions without any concrete reality.

Cunningham's dances offer the same potential for liberation that Watts describes above. Therefore, questions of meaning are resolved by making appropriate connections between Zen aesthetics and Cunningham's work – seeing the ways in which his dances allow human bodies moving in time and space to reflect the "cosmic dance," full of energy and spirit.

References

Addiss, Stephen. (1989) *The Art of Zen: Paintings and Calligraphy* by Japanese Monks 1600–1925. New York: Harry N. Abrams, Inc., p. 35

Anderson, Jack. (1975–76) Dances about everything and dances about some things. *Ballet Review* 5:4, pp. 56–60

Cage, John. (1968) A movement, a sound, a change of light. Concert Program for Brooklyn Academy of Music, UCR Dance Library

Capra, Fritjof. (1975) *The Tao of Physics: An Exploration of the Parallels Between Modern Physics and Eastern Mysticism.* New York: Bantam Book., p. 211

Copeland, Roger. (1983) Merce Cunningham and the politics of perception. Roger Copeland and Marshall Cohen, eds. *What is Dance?: Readings in Theory and Criticism.* Oxford: Oxford University Press, pp. 307–324

Croce, Arlene. (1980) Present at the creation. *The New Yorker.* March 10, pp. 145–149

Cunningham, Merce. 91955) The impermanent art. *Seven Arts #3*, Indian Hills, Colorado, pp. 71–73

————. (1976) Narrative for Event for television. Merrill Brockway, Director. WNET, *Dance in America*

————. (1985) *The Dancer and the Dance: Merce Cunningham in Conversation with Jaqueline Lesschaeve.* New York: Marion Boyars Publishers. pp. 97, 106, 129, ibid., 22

Kam'bayashi, Sumio. (1966) The old west meets the new east. *Ballet Review* 1:4, pp. 10–11

Ross, Nancy Wilson. (1966) *Three Ways of Asian Wisdom: Hindusim, Buddhism, Zen and Their Significance for the West.* New York: Simon and Schuster, pp. 183, 159

Seidensticker, Edward G., trans. (1960) *Snow Country* by Yasunari Kawabata, 1956. New York: Berkley Medallion Books, p. 7

Sparshott, Francis. (1985) Some dimensions of dance meaning. *The British Journal of Aesthetics* 25:2, Spring, pp. 101–114

Suzuki, Daisetz T. (1970) *Zen and Japanese Culture*, 1959. Princeton, New Jersey: Princeton University Press, pp. 219

Watts, Alan W. (1957) *The Way of Zen.* New York: Vintage Books, pp. 174–201

Wilhelm, Richard, and Cary F. Baynes, trans. (1967) *The I Ching: Or Book of Changes*, 1950. Princeton, New Jersey: Princeton University Press

Choreography and Dance, 1997, Vol. 4(3), p. 29–43
Photocopying permitted by license only

Visual Artists Design for the Merce Cunningham Dance Company, 1967–1970

Nelson Rivera

An account of the designs made by visual artists invited by Jasper Johns for the Merce Cunningham Dance Company, during the period 1967–1970. The study focuses on the interrelationship between Cunningham's concept of dance and the scene designs produced for his company. Both the aesthetic and the technical aspects of the designs are considered as they relate to the dances for which they were commissioned. Artists discussed are Frank Stella, designer for *Scramble* (1967); Andy Warhol, designer for *RainForest* (1968); Jasper Johns, after Marcel Duchamp, designer for *Walkaround Time* (1968); Robert Morris, designer for *Canfield* (1969); Bruce Nauman, designer for *Tread* (1970); Jasper Johns, designer for *Second Hand* (1970); and Neil Jenney, designer for *Objects* (1970).

KEY WORDS Cunningham, Merce; Johns, Jasper; scene design, contemporary dance, contemporary performance, contemporary art

> What we have done in our work is to bring together three separate elements in time and space, the music, the dance and the decor, allowing each one to remain independent. The three arts don't come from a single idea which the dance demonstrates, the music supports and the decor illustrates, but rather they are three separate elements each central to itself.
>
> – Merce Cunningham (1985, 137).

In 1967, Jasper Johns became the artistic advisor for the Merce Cunningham Dance Company. Previously, from 1954 to 1964, Robert Rauschenberg had been the resident designer. Rauschenberg's contributions to Cunningham's theatre were, as is well known, significant. Nevertheless, the differences between Rauschenberg and Johns in their respective approaches to scene design for the company became immediately noticeable.

The company at this time was in a less precarious financial situation than in the Rauschenberg years. It was partly for this reason that the new policy of commissioning designs from artists not associated with the company was made possible. As artistic advisor, Johns himself selected the invited artists, choosing, in his words,

> artists for whose work I have a high regard, who could understand a difference between theatre and studio, or gallery scale and space, (sometimes) who could work quickly. [Klosty, 85.]

It must be kept in mind that Cunningham's approach to collaboration in the theatre is not conventional. From the time of Rauschenberg's tenure in the company, the design element, as well as the music, has followed an independent course, finally meeting in performance rather than during the creation process. Whereas the close artistic relationship that developed between Cunningham and Rauschenberg became an important factor in their collaboration, the policy of

29

inviting artists, some of whom had little or no experience in the theatre, was an additional artistic and financial risk for the company.

Design for the Cunningham company posed a series of problems, some of which were common to any dance company, and some of which were rather unusual. Designers had to keep in mind that their designs had to be flexible enough to allow for the touring, the different stages the company would perform in, the ease for building, assembling, and packing of the set; the stage space also had to be free of physical obstacles to the dancers. Most important still, designers could not depend on Cunningham's explanations, as he insisted on the independence of the dance, the music, and the design.

It is this last aspect that makes the designing task for the artist both easier and harder; easier, because it frees the designer from the director's ideas, but harder, because the design, perhaps more so than the music, shapes the way the dance is perceived, as they are both visual and share the same space. A design could radically alter the choreography's look.

As would be expected, the invited artists had different attitudes towards the creation of their designs, sometimes taking into consideration the dance for which it had been made, sometimes not. What follows, then, is an account of the designs made by visual artists invited by Johns after Rauschenberg's departure from the Cunningham company.

Frank Stella, Designer for *Scramble*, 1967

Frank Stella had never designed a set before he was commissioned to design the set and costumes for Cunningham's *Scramble*. The artist saw a rehearsal of the, at that moment, still unfinished dance; after watching this rehearsal he asked questions regarding the height of dancers and the height and width of the stage. These measurements were considered for the design he produced, as well as Cunningham's suggestion that the set could, in some way, move.

The set Stella designed for *Scramble* consisted of six single color canvas bands (red, orange, yellow, green, blue, purple) held by metal frames at various heights. The longest band, which measured twenty-four feet wide, stood almost at floor level; the other bands proportionately narrowed as they rose, the tallest (standing eighteen feet up) being the narrowest (four feet wide). Each band was about two feet high.

Stella originally wanted cast-iron frames to hold the bands, but these turned out to be too heavy; aluminum was used instead. All the frames stood on casters, making each piece of the set moveable. In order to make the set pieces easy to travel with, the aluminum frames were built in sections which could be assembled by inserting one into another. The canvas bands were held tight to the frames with velcro strips.

The design allowed for different configurations in the placement of the pieces on stage. They could be scattered throughout, following no particular pattern, or stacked up against the backdrop with the lowest in front and the highest at the back. During the dance, the pieces could be moved to create new configurations and new spaces. The set was particularly suited for performances in open spaces such as gymnasiums, and it was used by Cunningham not only for performances of *Scramble*, but also for his *Events*.

Figure 1   L–R Merce Cunningham, Barbara Dilley, Gus Solomons Jr, Sandra Neels, (partially visible) Albert Reid, and Carolyn Brown in *Scramble*. Photo: Hervé Gloaguen.

Some sections of the dance were necessarily hidden from the audience's view, especially those that occurred behind the lowest bands. This was more the case when performances took place in proscenium theatres, in which the stage is usually higher than the audience; in gymnasiums and basketball courts, the audience usually looks down on the dancers.

The costumes designed by Stella consisted of leotards for the women and jumpsuits for the men. Each leotard was dyed in one of the six primary and secondary colors of the set's bands, plus black and white for Cunningham and Carolyn Brown, respectively.

Stella's design follows one of the principal characteristics of his art at that time, that is, the flatness of his painted canvases. Indeed, the set itself could be described as one of his stripe paintings cut up and distributed in space. While this flat quality reinforces the horizontality of the proscenium line, it also helps to define the space in all its dimensions, and to fill all available visual space, including that of the dancers. The flatness also creates a strong contrast with the lateral movements Cunningham devised for *Scramble* and which Stella took into consideration when he created the design.

In conventional proscenium stages, Stella's design allowed few diagonal movement paths for the dancers, owing to the frontality of the set, which, if moved diagonally, would cover side entrances from the wings. Also, sometimes the highest band could not be used because a particular stage was not high enough and hid it from view, making the design incomplete.

Figure 2   Merce Cunningham and Meg Harper in *RainForest*. Photo: James Klosty.

Andy Warhol, Designer for *RainForest*, 1968

Andy Warhol's decor for *RainForest* had a previous life of its own as a gallery installation called *Silver Clouds*. Cunningham, seeing the exhibition, was struck by the work's possibilities as a stage set, and asked Warhol for it.

The set consisted of twenty-five to thirty[1] "pillows" made of silver-colored mylar, measuring forty-two inches by fifty inches each. The pillows were filled with helium. Those floating at the back of the stage were secured to the floor by nearly invisible fishing lines with weights to prevent them from disappearing into the flies; other pillows were only half-filled with helium, and let loose to float around the stage among the dancers.

Warhol had no ideas for the costumes, his only suggestion being nudity. Since this was unacceptable to Cunningham, he gave Johns the following suggestion: "as if skin were torn" (Cunningham, 1985, 113). Johns had the dancers costumed in flesh-colored leotards, cutting holes in them while being worn by the dancers. Warhol's suggestion, thus, was realized, for the set's cold, shiny, metallic appearance reinforced the bare, vulnerable quality of the costumes.

The fact that Cunningham used an already completed art work which he felt suited his own, may account for the design's coherence with the choreographer's aesthetics. Cunningham aims for a dance that is non-focused, which uses the totality of the dancing space as a field in which all spaces are equally important, and all views of the dancers, front, back or side, equally interesting. This is precisely one of the reasons for his use of chance operations in his choreography.

Warhol's set shares these qualities with the choreography. The weightless, non-gravity-bound pillows give no sense of ideas such as "front," "back," "up," "down," or "side." *RainForest* was choreographed for only six dancers; there was no need for a large, open space for the dance. For this reason, the space, with the pillows lying around, appeared as if it were ready to configurate itself into something else at any time. The set looked unfixed, a feeling reinforced by the dancers' accidental encounters with the pillows. When these were touched or hit, they caused (or did not cause) a "domino effect" on the whole set. (In performances, it was not unusual for some pillows to cross the proscenium line into the orchestra pit and the auditorium.) The pillows also made sounds when hit, making an aural contribution of their own.

The set interacted with the dance by chance, at the same time maintaining independence from it. Cunningham may have had this in mind when the choreography was made, for sections of the dance had the dancers on the floor rolling in slow motion, or just lying or being thrown about by each other, not unlike the pillows.

This set appears to be well suited for touring (with the exception, perhaps, of the helium gas tank), and for its use in both proscenium and open stage theatres. The design is flexible enough to accommodate any configuration, but less so for storing backstage in theatres with limited wing space.

---

[1] *Time* magazine's critic counted twenty-five (May 24, 1968); Carolyn Brown counted thirty (Klosty, 30).

Figure 3   L–R Carolyn Brown, Valda Setterfield, Meg Harper, Gus Solomons Jr, and Merce Cunningham in *Walkaround Time*. Photo: Oscar Bailey.

Jasper Johns, After Marcel Duchamp's *The Bride Stripped Bare by Her Bachelors, Even...*, Designer for *Walkaround Time*, 1968

For his first major design for the Cunningham company,[2] Johns suggested the possibility of inviting Marcel Duchamp to contribute a set based on his work known as the *Large Glass*. He explained his ideas to Duchamp who agreed to it only if Johns would do the work. Thus, the concept for the set, as well as its realization, were both Johns's.

Johns's set consisted of seven air-filled transparent vinyl boxes, their rectangular shape held together by an aluminum frame. On the boxes, seven images from Duchamp's piece were silk-screened, one image on each box: *The Bride, The Milky Way, The Glider, The Cemetery of Uniforms, The Seven Sieves, The Ocular Witnesses,* and *The Chocolate Grinder*. The silk-screened images kept the same size relationship as in the painting, resulting in boxes of different sizes.

The images were silk-screened twice on the large sides of the boxes facing front. The image on the front panel was only an outline of Duchamp's images, while the one at the back was filled in and colored. This work, actually done by Johns himself, mirrored Duchamp's painting process in the lower section of the *Glass*,

---

[2]   Johns designed costumes for *Suite de Danses*, a television dance (Canadian television) in 1961.

where he had first outlined the figures with glued wire on the glass, and then colored them.[3]

Two boxes, those of the *Bride* and the *Milky Way*, were hung from the flies over the stage, for these images belong to the upper panel of the *Large Glass*. The remaining five boxes stood on the stage, isolated and spaced to allow for the dancers' movements. Duchamp's sole request about the design was that the boxes be assembled at some point in the dance in the actual order of the images as they appear in the *Large Glass*. This was accomplished at the end of the dance, close to the *Bride* and *Milky Way* boxes hanging at the back of the stage.

The boxes were lightweight; this enabled the dancers to move some of them at various moments in the dance, as well as for the closing sequence. Even though the actual set was not seen by Cunningham until the day before the first performance, Johns had provided him cardboard substitutes for the rehearsals. Cunningham had found that the boxes restricted the movements in space, so he choreographed accordingly, with entrances and movements done mostly laterally.

On those occasions in which the choreography made use of the boxes, it was mainly as "frames" for specific actions;[4] an example of this was the lifting of the small *Ocular Witnesses* box to frame the head of a dancer. At least three Cunningham solos took place behind the three largest boxes, Cunningham limiting himself to the area behind each box. Some movements also echoed the stage design: A dancer would sometimes freeze in place; other dancers would pick him up and carry him across the stage as if he were a box, the dancer never losing his frozen position while being carried.

Although not all of the choreography was concerned with Duchamp, it did in fact refer to some of his works at various moments in the dance. One of Cunningham's solos consisted of running in place while changing clothes, a reference to the *Nude Descending a Staircase*, as well as to Duchamp's lifelong interest in motion and the nude. Another reference was made to Duchamp's participation in the "Entr'acte" film for the Dadaist *Relâche* ballet (1924); this took the form of an "intermission" in which the dancers took a break on stage for seven minutes. Cunningham referred to this segment as a "readymade," as indeed it was. Some lighting effects also made reference to specific ideas found in Duchamp's work, such as the lighting that caused the hanging boxes to cast their images' shadows on the backdrop.[5]

Walkaround Time was an unusual addition to Cunningham's repertoire in that the choice of the scene design (Duchamp's *Large Glass*) determined, among other things, the choice of movements in the choreography as well as the sounds for the music score, thus resulting in a more coherent work.[6]

---

[3] Johns was familiar with this medium as he had been making some of his own drawings on plastic since 1962. See Rosenthal and Fine, 174.

[4] These "frames" were used very much in the same way Richard Foreman uses his in his theatre productions.

[5] Shadows appear in a number of Duchamp works, including his 1918 painting *Tu m'*.

[6] The music included, among other things, superimposed readings of Duchamp's notes for the *Large Glass*.

Figure 4   Merce Cunningham Dance Company in *Canfield*. Photo: James Klosty.

Robert Morris, Designer for *Canfield*, 1969

Robert Morris was already experienced in dance work when Johns commissioned from him a design for Cunningham. He was not only a visual artist, but a dance performer and creator of a number of dance and theatre performances. Morris's first suggestion for the design was a body makeup that changed colors when the temperature changed. This was not accepted. Morris subsequently gave Johns a set of instructions for the design that was finally used in the evening-length *Canfield*. Apparently, no plans or drawings were prepared by Morris, nor did he take care of the design's realization.

The set consisted of a pillar hanging from a track right next to the prosceniun opening. Inside the pillar, unseen to the audience, was a set of strong lights focused on the backdrop. The pillar, by means of a motor, moved from side to side of the stage at a constant speed, illuminating the stage and the backdrop as it passed. The number of times the pillar would cross the stage to either side depended on the length of the dance, which varied from performance to performance, and the width of the stage. At various points during the dance, choreographic notes and music score notes were projected on the backdrop from the auditorium; these projections were also caught by the moving pillar's surface (painted gray), seen by the audience, and obliterated by the pillar's lights on the gray backdrop.

Morris wanted the backdrop and the costumes coated with the reflective paint used for highway traffic signs. The idea was that the backdrop and the dancers would light up and "flare" when the pillar illuminated them. Johns himself painted both the backdrop and the costumes according to Morris's instructions. The "flare" effect, however, never worked out as intended, for the light source had to be close to the viewer's eye in order for the reflection to be seen. Only if each audience member had a light beam would it be seen.[7] As a result, the most noticeable light change in the costumes and backdrop was their changing from gray to brilliant white.

The stage space was very wide, since the legs or borders were not used, and low general lighting was kept on the stage throughout the performance. Even though separated from the set, the dancers were not oblivious to it. They had to avoid looking at the harsh, blinding lights coming from the pillar, which could cause accidents.

With *Canfield*, Cunningham returned to his practice of working independently of the designer and the composer (which had not been the case of *Walkaround Time*). Morris's design, however, brought back Rauschenberg's practice of integrating the set, costumes and lighting in the design concept,[8] and was an attempt even to include the choreography and the music in the design by way of projections. At the same time, both the set and the dance maintained their independence from each other, for they did not share the same space.

Morris's design was meant for a proscenium theatre; it probably would not work in spaces where the audience sits on more than one side. Touring with it was not easy either, for the unassembled pillar took much crate space. Also, it had to be adjusted every time to the proscenium height of each different theatre.

Bruce Nauman, Designer for *Tread*, 1970

Bruce Nauman's set for Cunningham consisted of ten floor-stand industrial fans laid in a row along the footlights of a proscenium theatre, raised at different heights. The fans were all turned on; five of them oscillated, while the remaining five, alternatively, stood still. Audience members sitting in the front rows could feel the breeze coming from the stage. This design kept the stage free for the dance, and did not attempt to interact with the dancers except for purely marginal aspects: there was the same number of fans as of dancers, and the fans as well as the dancers were in motion.

It could be argued that this set was not made for the dance, but rather for the audience. Nauman's design intensified the awareness of the proscenium line, the separation of the stage and the auditorium, by placing a barrier between them,[9] a barrier that is, nonetheless, bridged by the visual transparency of the fans and the invisible breeze that reaches the audience.

---

[7] Carolyn Brown recalls that the dancers could sometimes see the intended effect since they were close to the pillar (as told at the *Merce Cunningham and the New Dance* symposium, 7 March 1897, New York City).

[8] Examples of this are the designs for *Nocturnes* (1956), *Summerspace* (1958), and *Story* (1963).

[9] Compare to Brecht's use of the half-curtain and Richard Foreman's lines across the stage.

Figure 5   Merce Cunningham Dance Company in *Tread*. Photo: James Klosty.

As with Morris's set, Nauman's was strongly proscenium-oriented, and probably would not work as well in other spaces. Unlike Morris's, it was easy to install, and comparatively inexpensive to tour with, as Nauman suggested the fans could be rented instead of bought (van Bruggen, 240, n. 9).[10]

Jasper Johns, designer for *Second Hand*, 1970

Johns's next design for the company was for one of Cunningham's and John Cage's most cherished projects, a dance choreographed to Erik Satie's *Socrate*.[11] *Second Hand* was divided into three parts: part one was a solo for Cunningham, part two a duet for Cunningham and Carolyn Brown, and part three was for the full

---

[10]   Both *Canfield* and *Tread* were taken on tour to Europe at the same time, along with *Second Hand*, which has no set (Klosty, 138).

[11]   As is well known, Cunningham choreographed the dance to Cage's arrangement for two pianos of *Socrate*. When the rights to the music were denied, Cage composed a solo piano piece keeping *Socrate*'s rhythmical structure, but changing the melody through chance operations. Cage's piece is called *Cheap Imitation*.

Figure 6   Merce Cunningham Dance Company in *Second Hand*. Photo: James Klosty.

company of ten dancers (including Brown and Cunningham). Cunningham remained on stage during the whole thirty-five-minute dance.

Contrary to the artists he had previously commissioned designs from, Johns
provided costumes but no set, leaving the stage completely bare for the dance,
which was performed in front of a dark backdrop. The costumes consisted of leotards and tights for the women, and tights and long-sleeved shirts, with V-necks
and pointed collars, for the men.

Costumes were dyed by Johns. Each dancer wore a single-colored costume which
turned into another color at the edges of the left arm and leg; this other color was
the main color worn by another dancer. At the end of the dance, when the dancers
assembled for the final bow, a color spectrum was fully revealed in the following
manner, from left to right:[12]

(male) magenta to Chinese red;
(female) red to deep orange;
(male) orange to orange-yellow;
(female – Carolyn Brown) yellow-orange to yellow;

---

[12]   Color spectrums are found in several of Johns's paintings.

(male – Cunningham) yellow to yellow-green;
(female) yellow-green to green;
(male) green to blue-green;
(female) blue-green to blue;
(male) blue to violet;
(female) violet to magenta.

Cunningham and Brown wore the brightest-colored costumes as they had solos in the first two parts of the dance.

Johns has commented on his belief that sets are not necessary for dance;[13] however, his decision not to use a set for *Second Hand* satisfied not only Cunningham's needs (a large space for the full company to dance in) but, most significantly, was in accord with Satie's composition on which the dance was based. The music had been appropriately described by the composer as "white and pure like the Antique" (Volta, 154), unfolding in utmost tranquillity. Johns's (non) set, an expansive emptiness, follows this concept of a "degree zero" music. The costumes also submit to this idea, for, as is known, the sum of the colors in the spectrum results in white light. Clearly, Johns's designs virtually followed *Socrate*. Although it went largely unnoticed at the time, *Second Hand* was one of Cunningham's most coherent pieces in terms of the close relationship between the music, the choreography, and the design.[14]

While *Second Hand* did not remain long in Cunningham's repertoire, Cunningham's opening solo was included in the CBS Camera Three program "A Video Event" (1974).[15]

Neil Jenney, designer for *Objects*, 1970

Primarily recognized as a painter, Neil Jenney was in fact better known as a sculptor when Johns asked him to design for the dance company. Although Jenney had not worked in the theatre before, he had, in 1968, described his sculptures as "theatrical." In his words, "the activity among the physical presences of the items and the events they realize, provided they exist together, is theatrical. This goes beyond the visual image" (University Art Museum, 44). This concept provided the basis for the designs Jenney produced for Cunningham.

Jenney designed four tripod-shaped structures of various heights (roughly around twelve feet) made out of lightweight metal tubing. Pieces of black cloth were used to partially drape the structures in random patterns. All structures had wheels on one of their three legs, and the remaining legs were covered with rubber caps in order to protect the dance floor. The wheels enabled the dancers to

---

[13]   See Klosty, 85.

[14]   Recent examples would certainly include the 1977 Cage-Cunningham-Morris Graves collaboration entitled *Inlets*, and the Cage-Cunningham-Mark Lancaster collaboration *Roaratorio* (1983).

[15]   Carolyn Brown left the company in 1972. Most of the works in which she played a significant role were dropped from the repertoire.

Figure 7 L–R Chase Robinson, Sandra Neels, Carolyn Brown, and Douglas Dunn in *Objects*. Photo: James Klosty.

carry the structures, wheelbarrow-style, in, out, and around the stage during the dance.[16]

The structures, looking like unstable, askew scaffoldings, were strictly composed of diagonal lines.[17] These diagonal lines produced a number of diversely shaped three- and four-sided frames through which the dance was seen. As the structures were wheeled about, these frames periodically redefined the audience's view as well as the dancing space. Visual obstructions caused by the draped cloths also modified the audience's perception of the dance. The design thus shared Cunningham's aesthetics of changeability.

Objects did not remain long in the company's repertoire. Although it accommodates to both proscenium and open stages, Jenney's set was not used again.

Cunningham's insistence in keeping his collaborators' work independent of his own poses a good deal of problems which, as may be seen from the previous seven examples, can yield a number of exceptional solutions. As different as their designs were, the six artists discussed shared at least three main characteristics in their designs:

> First, the bringing over of their respective aesthetic ideas into Cunningham's work without disguising his or theirs.

> Second, the use of the totality of the space as opposed to only that of the wings and the backdrop, as is the conventional practice in designs for the dance.

> Third, all seven designs included motion (either of their own or with the dancers' help), intensifying the experience of the dance, which is motion.

Finally, all the artists addressed themselves, in one way or another, to one of the twentieth-century theatre's most recurrent concerns – the relationship between the performance and the spectator.

Warmest thanks to Carolyn Brown, Douglas Dunn, David Vaughan, William Fetterman, Jasper Johns, and most specially to Michael Kirby.

References

Atlas, Charles. (1973) *Walkaround Time*. Color film.
Barnes, Clive. (1969) Dance: The Golden Sound of Silence. *New York Times*, 16 April, 32.
————. (1970a) Dance: Is Cunningham Too Restricted? *New York Times*, 29 November, 18.
————. (1970b) Dance: New Cunningham. "Second Hand" Offered at Brooklyn Academy. *New York Times*, 10 January, 36.
————. (1970c) Dance: New Cunningham. "Tread" Gets Premiere as the Season Opens. *New York Times*, 6 January, 49.

---

[16]   The choreography was connected to the set in other ways as well. For example, a dancer would carry another dancer on stage; those movements prompted reviewers' comments such as "[the] dancers are sometimes treated like objects..." (Jowitt 1970b).

[17]   This concern with instability is evident in Jenney's installations such as *The David Whitney Piece* (1968), with its use of a three-legged table, and *The Noah Goldowsky Piece*, (1969). See University Art Museum, 23–25.

CBS Camera Three (1979) *A Video Event*. New York: CBS/TV

Cunningham, Kitty. (1971) The Merce Cunningham Dance Company at the Brooklyn Academy. *Dance and Dancers*, 22, 2: 49.

Cunningham, Merce. (1968) *Changes/Notes on Choreography*. New York: Something Else Press.

————. (1985) *The Dancer and the Dance*, in conversation with Jacqueline Lesschaeve. London: Marion Boyars.

Dance in America. (1977) *Merce Cunningham and Dance Company: Event for Television*. New York: WNET-13.

Emily Lowe Gallery. (1974) *Diaghilev/Cunningham*, exhibition catalogue. Hempstead, Long Island: Hofstra University.

Glueck, Grace. (1968) Jump Suits and Silver Pillows. *New York Times*, 12 May, 31.

Highwater, Jamake. (1985) *Dance: Rituals of Experience*. New York: Alfred van der Marck Editions.

Hodgson, Moira. (1976) *Quintet: Five American Dance Companies*. New York: William Morrow and Company, Inc.

Johnston, Jill. (1968) Okay Fred. *The Village Voice*, 23 May, 32–33.

Jowitt, Deborah. (1969) Dance: Solitary Games. *The Village Voice*, 24 April, 26.

————. (1970a) Dance: Cedar Shrine, Doe Stands C. *The Village Voice*, 15 January, 29.

————. (1970b) Dance: Pleasure and Choler. *The Village Voice*, 19 November, 35.

————. (1977c) *Dance Beat: Selected Views and Reviews 1967–1976*. New York: Marcel Dekker, Inc.

Kisselgoff, Anna. (1970) To Merce Cunningham, Dance is Reflection of Today. *New York Times*, 10 November, 54.

Klosty, James, ed. (1975) *Merce Cunningham*. New York: E. P. Dutton.

Lehman College Arts Gallery. (1987) *Merce Cunningham and his Collaborators*, exhibition catalogue. New York: The City University of New York.

Livet, Anne, ed. (1978) *Contemporary Dance*. New York: Abbeville Press, Inc.

McDonagh, Don. (1970a) New Dance Limns Joy and Sadness: Cunningham's "Objects" Uses Imbalance as Device. *New York Times*, 11 November, 41.

————. (1970b) *The Rise and Fall of and Rise of Modern Dance*. New York: E.P. Dutton and Co., Inc.

Percival, John. (1970) Cunningham in Paris. *Dance and Dancers*, 21, 10: 42–44.

Public Broadcast Laboratory. (1969) *RainForest*. Color film.

Rosenthal, Nan, and Ruth E. Fine. (1990) *The Drawings of Jasper Johns*. New York: Thames and Hudson.

Seigel, Marcia. (1970) Come in, Earth, Are You There? *Arts in Society*, Spring/Summer, 70–76.

Snell, Michael. (1971) Cunningham and the Critics. *Ballet Review*, 3, 6: 16–39.

State University of New York. (1987) *Merce Cunningham and the New Dance*, a festival with symposia. New York: State University of New York.

Terry, Walter. (1970) Merce in Antic Mood. *Saturday Review*, 24 January, 40.

The Dance: Having a Ball in Brooklyn. (1968) *Time*, 24 May, 86.

Tomkins, Calvin. (1976) *The Bride and the Bachelors*. New York: Penguin Books.

van Bruggen, Coosje (1988) *Bruce Nauman*. New York: Rizzoli International Publications, Inc.

Vaughan, David. (1980) The Art of Working with Artists. *The Sunday Times Magazine*, 13 April, 52.

Volta, Ornella. (1989) *Satie Seen Through His Letters*. Trans. Michael Bullock. London: Marion Boyars.

Willis, John. (1970) *Dance World 1970: 1969–1970 Season*. Vol. 5. New York: Crown Publishers, Inc.

————. (1971) *Dance World 1971: 1970–1971 Season*. Vol. 6. New York: Crown Publishers, Inc.

Choreography and Dance, 1997, Vol. 4(3), p. 45–49
Photocopying permitted by license only

The Roles of David Tudor in the Early Repertory of the Merce Cunningham Dance Company

John Holzaepfel
Fort Atkinson, Wisconsin

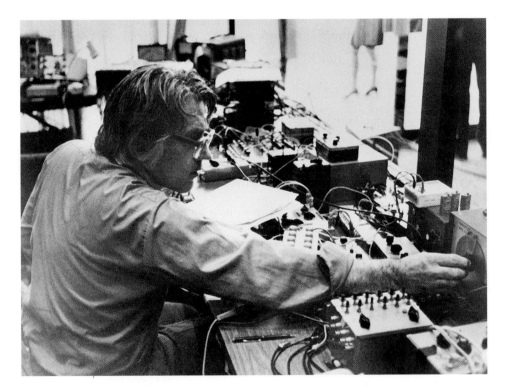

Figure 1 David Tudor.

David Tudor's importance to the histories of the Merce Cunningham Dance Company and of John Cage's music is well known but has never been explained. This is a puzzling omission, for Tudor's contribution as accompanist for the Company, from its inception at Black Mountain College in the summer of 1953 to the present, has been not only indispensable but unique. The paper offers a partial account of both of these qualities as they obtained in Tudor's early work with Cunningham and Cage.

The reputation Tudor eventually acquired as the foremost pianist of the radical wing of the avant garde obscures his deep interest in the little known and rarely performed piano literature of the 19th and early 20th centuries. As accompanist for the new Cunningham Company, Tudor found opportunity to perform some of this literature with such Cunningham dances as *Banjo* and *Dime a Dance*.

Furthermore, Tudor was a conduit between the newest music and the Cunningham Dance Company's repertory. Frequently, Cunningham attended Tudor's solo recitals, and a number of the pieces he heard on these occasions found their way into his dance repertory. Long before he turned away from the piano and began to sign his name to his own works of live electronic music, David Tudor in more than one way furnished the Merce Cunningham Dance Company with some of its most characteristic music.

KEY WORDS: Tudor, David; accompaniment; piano literature; dance repertory

The association of Merce Cunningham and John Cage hardly requires explanation. Having known one another since 1938, they began in 1942 a continuous collaboration based on the mutual development of ideas compatible to both dance and music. In addition to his independent compositional and performance activities, Cage served as Cunningham's accompanist for the remainder of the 1940s.

In the early 1950s, David Tudor entered this configuration. Tudor's importance to the histories of the Cunningham Dance Company and of Cage's music is well known and has been acknowledged by both dancer and composer. Nonetheless, Tudor's place in the configuration has not been explained. This is a puzzling omission, for Tudor's contribution as accompanist for the Company, from its inception at Black Mountain College in the summer of 1953 to the present, has been not only indispensable but unique. The following offers a partial account of both of these qualities as they obtained in Tudor's early work with Cunningham and Cage.

Tudor's work for Cunningham actually predates the formation of the Cunningham Dance Company by several years. In late 1949, Cage asked Tudor to make a rehearsal recording of the piano reduction of Ben Weber's *Ballet*, Op. 26, composed for Cunningham's dance *Pool of Darkness* (the reduction was too difficult for Cage himself, at that time still Cunningham's accompanist).[1] But it was almost a year later, when Cage arranged the American premiere of the Second Piano Sonata of Pierre Boulez, given by Tudor on 17 December 1950, that an active Cage-Tudor association began. This is to say that Cage had found in Tudor not only a pianist superbly equipped to perform new music of the most demanding technical virtuosity. For Tudor was more than merely receptive to the radically innovative music of Cage and the composers he supported – Morton Feldman, Christian Wolff, and, later, Earle Brown: he was in a very real sense a necessary and effective cause of its composition.

---

[1]   Morton Feldman said that he introduced Tudor to Cage, an account sometimes repeated by Cage himself. But Feldman and Cage met on 26 January 1950, following a performance, at Carnegie Hall, of the Webern Symphony, Op. 21; by that time, the premiere of *Pool of Darkness* had already taken place at Hunter College Playhouse on 15 January. Cage and Tudor were, in fact, introduced by Jean Erdman.

This confusion over the exact dates of the beginnings of the friendship should not surprise: even Cunningham did not know it was Tudor who made the Weber recording until 1989. I have untangled the sequence of events in "The Tudor Factor", in *John Cage Anarchic Harmony*, ed. S. Schädler and W. Zimmermann (Mainz: B. Schott, 1992), pp. 43–53.

By the time he was first approached by Cage, Tudor, though not yet 24 years old, was already an experienced accompanist. Having moved to New York from his native Philadelphia in 1947, he frequently took part in concerts of new music, but he earned his living by accompanying such dancers as Mary Anthony and Joseph Gifford, Midi Garth, Merle Marsicano, Katherine Litz, and Jean Erdman. In this area, as in his concert performances, his playing was highly regarded from the beginning, as is evidenced in a recollection of one of his early colleagues, Jean Erdman:

> [It was] like magic. What a wonderful thing it was to dance when he played the piano. He played at the peak of the music, and at the peak of where the rhythm and movement matched that of the dance. His relationship to piano sound was unique; he created the sound in its perfect rhythmic location. The texture, the quality of sound, the way he touched the keys – treating the piano both as percussive and melodic – made such a difference to a dancer. It was not so much the listening aspect as the kinaesthetic; it would increase the expressive energy. It really sparked the 'goddess of dance' in you.[2]

The reputation Tudor eventually acquired as the foremost pianist of the radical wing of the avant garde obscures another part of his musical disposition. This was his deep interest in the little known and rarely performed music of the past, in particular, the forgotten piano literature of the 19th and early 20th centuries.[3] His usual venue for performing this music was as accompanist for singers and instrumentalists, on whose recital programs he would sometimes insert a solo piano piece, usually by Busoni, a composer to whom Tudor retained a special devotion originally kindled by his teachers, Irma and Stefan Wolpe. But as accompanist for the new Cunningham Company, Tudor also found opportunity to perform some of the rarely played music of the past.[4]

The music for the Company's first season was not yet entirely made up of new works.[5] The repertory for the New York season at the Theatre de Lys at the end of 1953 included several earlier Cunningham dances (to music either by Cage or by one of Cage's most important predecessors, Erik Satie). But although the dances performed at Black Mountain College the previous summer were new, they were not all dances with contemporary music.

During that summer of 1953, a time that marked the birth of the Cunningham Dance Company, Cunningham wanted to make a dance to American music, and asked Tudor for suggestions. The result was *Banjo*, a dance to the work of the same

---

[2] Jean Erdman, telephone conversation and interview with author, New York, 10 and 15 March 1992.

[3] Harold C. Schonberg briefly discusses this aspect of Tudor in "The Far-Out Pianist", *Harper's Magazine* (June 1960), p. 54. Schoenberg's informal profile remains the only full-length (i.e. 6 pages) essay devoted solely to Tudor's career as a pianist.

[4] At one time, early in his career, Tudor considered the idea of including both contemporary and rarely heard earlier works in his recital repertory, but soon rejected the idea as "too competitive". David Tudor, interview with author, Stony Point, N.Y., 3 August 1992.

[5] Cunningham continued to dance with earlier music as late as 1957, when he choreographed *Picnic Polka* to Gottschalk's *Ses Yeux*. This dance was a companion piece to *Banjo*.

name by Louis Moreau Gottschalk (1829–69), one of Tudor's special delights.[6] For that first season, Cunningham also presented Tudor with his idea of a collection of brief dances, each structured within a metrical framework (though not oriented to metric beats), leaving it to Tudor to provide whatever music he wished. This time, the result was *Dime a Dance*, described in the program as "a grab-bag of dance" and requiring the entire company's availability on stage to perform which-ever seven of thirteen possible dances came up on cards drawn by members of the audience, who would pay ten cents for the privilege (this dance was never popular with the dancers, whose efforts in preparing many of the dances were, of course, for nought).[7]

The music Tudor selected for *Dime a Dance* was by such a variety of composers that the credits on the program read "The Whole World." Some of the selections – Debussy's *Rêverie*, Beethoven's Bagatelle in B minor, from Op. 126 – were familiar enough.[8] Some, like Moszkowski's *morceau de fantaisie, La Jongleuse*, Op. 52, had at one time been popular encore or salon pieces. The remaining fourteen compositions included pieces by Gottschalk (*Radieuse* [*grande valse*] and *Souvenir de Porto Rico*, for the dances "The Waltz" and "The Lunge"), Alkan (*Gros Temps*, from *Les Mois*, for "The Insect"), and Hába (*Tango*, for the dance of the same name), and others obscure beyond belief (such items as the *Tarentelle*, Op. 4, of Génari Karganoff, a *Prelude* by Lund Skabo, Ludwig Stasny's *Kutschke-Polka*, and the *Springtime of Youth* Gavotte by Charles Breton). In all cases, they were works that Tudor had long known and believed worth keeping alive.

Finally, a deeper point needs to be made. Just as he was more than a performer for the newest music, Tudor was more than a superior accompanist for the Cunningham Dance Company. Cunningham frequently attended Tudor's solo re-citals and, like the composers themselves, was astonished by Tudor's playing. Of one series of recitals, he said:

> I remember those programs in Steinway Hall that David gave when he played pieces by John, Earle [Brown], Morty [Feldman]. And I have such a vivid impression of every single piece being different. Absolutely every single piece had its character. It was just amazing. He gave a very distinct quality to each piece.
>
> He was so remarkable to watch play. At that time he wore a dress suit – tails. He would often have to reach into the piano; with all this [other] regu-lar playing, then being all over the piano, so to speak. And I was absolutely struck by... the only word I can use is 'grace.' The way he would do this, flicking the tails out of the way. It was astonishing, the amount of energy displayed with the minimal effort. The way he made fortes – very, very loud

---

[6]   Cunningham has frequently told the story of Tudor's playing of this work as sounding "like sixty banjos going at once".

[7]   See Mary Emma Harris, *The Arts at Black Mountain College* (Cambridge: MIT Press, 1987), p. 238.
The selection procedure was modified for the company's New York debut the following winter, when the dances were selected through chance operations in the form of seven pantomimes (infor-mation from program in the David Tudor Collection).

[8]   The Beethoven Bagatelle was the music for Cunningham's solo dance "The Eclectic", a number he would often perform as an encore if it had not come up in the selection process.

sounds – you could watch and you couldn't see how anyone could make such a loud, distinct, clear sound with such little visible effort.[9]

Cunningham not only marvelled at Tudor's playing of new works. A number of the pieces he heard at these recitals found their way into his dance repertory. Among them were *Untitled Solo* (1953; music: Christian Wolff, *For Piano I*), *Galaxy* (1956; music: Earle Brown, *Four Systems*), *Lavish Escapade* (1956; music: Wolff, *For Piano II*), *Antic Meet* (1958; music: Cage, *Concert for Piano and Orchestra*), and *Night Wandering*: (1958; music: Bo Nilsson, *Bewegungen, Quantitäten, Schlagfiguren*). In turn (and I have alluded to this above) the composers of these works often acknowledged that without the stimulation and challenge of Tudor's skill and imagination, their compositions would not have come into existence in the first place. Long before he turned away from the piano and began to sign his name to his own works of live electronic music, David Tudor in more than one way furnished the Merce Cunningham Dance Company with some of its most characteristic music.

---

[9] Merce Cunningham, interview with author, 31 July 1989, New York City.

Choreography and Dance, 1997, Vol. 4(3), p. 51–58
Photocopying permitted by license only

Electronic Music for the Merce Cunningham Dance Company

Gordon Mumma

Electronic music appeared in the work of Merce Cunningham as early as 1952, and its use increased into the 1970s, by which time it had become predominant in his company's performances. The principal innovators in this field were John Cage, the company's music director, and David Tudor, company musician from its inception in 1953, who himself began to compose innovative electronic scores in the late 1960s. Both Cage and Tudor were responsible for devising custom-made instruments to play these scores. Other musicians also contributed to the development, and have continued to do so up to the present time.

KEY WORDS   Live electronic music, magnetic tape, John Cage, Merce Cunningham, collaboration.

Introduction

Electronic music resources appeared in the work of Merce Cunningham as early as 1952. The use of electronic music increased into the 1970s, by which time electronic music had become predominant in the Cunningham Dance Company performances. A major impetus for the development of electronic music resources in the Cunningham Dance Company milieu came from music director John Cage.

Cage's pioneering use of electronic musical resources began in 1939, with his now-classic percussion ensemble composition *Imaginary Landscape # 1*, in which he employed variable-speed phonograph turntables as performed musical instruments. Cage's artistic innovation with electronic technology continued into the 1940s (e.g., with music for a CBS Radio Drama production of Kenneth Patchen's *City with a Slouch Hat*).

Early electronic-music and magnetic tape

In the Cunningham repertory the first notable work to use electronic music resources was *Collage* (1952), choreographed to excerpts from the *Symphonie pour un homme seul* by Pierre Schaeffer and Pierre Henry. This landmark of "musique concrète" was composed using sounds recorded and edited on disk; in the Cunningham Dance Company performances the music was played using a tape recording.

In 1952 the tape recorder had been in general use for only a few years. Since then it has become perhaps the most common way of presenting music for modern dance (and even ballet) performances; the procedure is called "canned music." But canned music has been a rare practice in the Cunningham Dance Company. Most of the Cunningham music, whether for conventional instruments or using electronic resources, has been performed live. The few exceptions have been extraordinary, such as Conlon Nancarrow's *Rhythmic Studies for Player Piano*, to which Merce Cunningham choreographed *Crises* (1960).

Another work that used original music made for magnetic tape, *Winterbranch* (1964, La Monte Young's *2 Sounds (April 1960)*) received special notoriety. The theatrical impact depended on relentlessly abrasive sound, practical because of the tape medium, and was supported by Robert Rauschenberg's stark and unpredictable lighting.

An ensemble of tape recorders was used as performed instruments in the music for *Field Dances* (1963, John Cage's *Variations IV*). Further, both the choreography and music for *Field Dances* shared a structural characteristic; they were modular. Musical sequences were recorded and retrieved from magnetic tape, choreographic sequences were learned and "retrieved" from memory by the dancers. The overall structure of *Field Dances* varied from one performance to the next; during each performance the dancers independently chose the choreographic sequences and the musicians chose the recorded sound sequences. Such relatively extreme freedom-of-choice for the dancers was uncommon in Cunningham's work, though in that same year it was also a feature of *Story* (1963, music by Toshi Ichiyanagi).

Amplication and custom-built electronics

By the late 1950s Cage had composed several works using amplified small sounds, performed often with pianist David Tudor. These "small sounds," usually inaudible to an audience without amplification, were from live acoustical sources (piano, percussion, invented or found instruments).

Two Cunningham repertory works of 1958 used amplification: *Antic Meet* (John Cage's *Concert for Piano and Orchestra*) and *Night Wandering* (Bo Nilsson's *Bewegungen, Quantitäten, Schlagfiguren*). The spectacularly virtuoso piano solo for *Night Wandering*, performed by David Tudor, was amplified to reveal quiet, pedal-sustained resonances of the instrument, and magnify the higher partials of the piano sonority. The result was a surreal timbral brilliance appropriate to Tudor's shattering keyboard virtuosity.

Electronic amplification and equalization, also used in *Aeon* (1961, Cage's *Atlas Eclipticalis with Winter Music*), was done with a rapidly burgeoning assortment of small equipment – transducers, preamplifiers, equalizers, and mixers. This equipment collection became a space– and time-consuming menagerie for Cage and Tudor.

Electronic music systems and live-electronic music

Undeterred by the logistical challenge of yet more electronic equipment, Cage and Cunningham collaborated on the large-scale multi-media work *Variations V* (1965). This work employed an electronic performance system that integrated the music, dance, and aspects of the lighting. With the technical assistance of Bell Laboratories engineers, electronic designer Robert Moog, and the collaboration of visual artists Nam June Paik and Stan VanDerBeek, the stage was rigged with a system of photo-electric and capacitive electronic sensors, and sound-transducers were attached to the decor. This sensor system monitored the physical locations and movements of the dancers as they performed Cunningham's choreography. The musicians in the orchestra pit used electronic signals from these on-stage sensors to articulate the musical sounds from a sprawling ensemble of tape recorders and

Figure 1 *Variations V*
Foreground: L–R John Cage, David Tudor, and Gordon Mumma. Rear: L–R Carolyn Brown, Merce Cunningham, and Barbara Dilley. Photo: Hervé Gloaguen.

radio receivers. Further, the sounds of the dancers and their manipulation of stage decor was amplified with the use of on-stage transducers.

Beginning with *Variations* V, and continuing into the 1990s, the development of live-performance electronic systems unique to each musical work became a characteristic feature of the Cunningham repertory. For *Place* (1966, Gordon Mumma's *Mesa*) the sounds of Tudor's bandoneon performance were drastically altered by a system of electronic sound-modulators. For *RainForest* (1968, Tudor's *Rainforest*) an ensemble of unique electro-acoustic instruments, designed by Tudor, were performed in ecologically dependent interaction. For *TV Rerun* (1972, Mumma's *Telepos*) the dancers wore accelerometer belts integrated with a radio-telemetry system. The music resulted directly from the accelerations of the dancers as they performed Cunningham's choreography.

Earlier "outside" composers

From in the late 1960s a growing diversity of composers were invited to make music for the Cunningham repertory. Many responded by developing the live-

Figure 2   Rehearsing for first performance of *Place*, Fondation Maeght, St Paul de Vence, France, August 1966. Foreground: John Cage, right; rear: Gordon Mumma, left; Merce Cunningham and dancers. Photo: Hervé Gloaguen.

performance aspects of unique electronic music systems, or configurations that integrated electronic with acoustical instruments.

Scramble (1967, Toshi Ichiyanagi's *Activities for Orchestra*), *Walkaround Time* (1968, David Behrman's *for nearly an hour*), and *Canfield* (1969, Pauline Oliveros's *In Memoriam Nicola Tesla – Cosmic Engineer*) each required unique and elaborate interactive electronic-music systems that could be exhausting in preparation and performance. The transportation logistics of the Cunningham Dance Company on tour became formidable – sometimes there was a greater quantity of musical equipment than stage decor and costumes. Thus it was a delectable pleasure to perform the music for *Objects* (1970, Alvin Lucier's *Vespers*) in which the total musical equipment was four hand-held echo-sounders that could be transported in a single attaché case.

Collaborative compositions and Events

This live electronic-music production depended upon creative collaboration of composers, musicians, engineers, technicians, and, at times, even the dancers. Historical examples of effective interdisciplinary arts collaboration are not common, and are particularly rare when the musical concepts and results are innovative and radical, as with the Cunningham Dance Company. Even the example of composers collaborating on a single work is unusual in the art music traditions. Perhaps because of their ongoing involvement (and commitment) with innovative musical technology, collaboration between composers became a fruitful and celebrated characteristic of the Cunningham Dance Company.

Composer collaboration was nourished by the production of one-time-only *Events* (from 1964 onwards), and by projects such as the television-film *Assemblage* (1968, produced by KQED, San Francisco) with music co-composed by Cage, Mumma, and Tudor. The first co-composed or collaborative repertory works appeared in the early 1970s, with *Signals* (1970) and *Landrover* (1972), which also had music by Cage, Mumma, and Tudor. Each of these two works used a different collaborative procedure that the composers had agreed upon prior to making the music.

Later "outside" composers

From the mid-1960s onward the composer-performers using electronic resources and touring with the Cunningham Dance Company included (besides Cage, Tudor, and Mumma) David Behrman, Martin Kalve, Takehisa Kosugi, and Michael Pugliese. From the 1980s onwards musician-technicians, such as John Fullemann, Rob Miller, John D.S. Adams, and D'Arcy Philip Gray also toured with the group. Other composers who used electronic resources in their music for the Cunningham Dance Company include (besides those mentioned previously) Maryanne Amacher, Robert Ashley, Larry Austin, Jon Gibson, John King, Ivan Tcherepnin, Yasunao Tone, Christian Wolff, and Emanuel Dimas de Melo Pimenta.

Musical issues in context and consequence

With the background of the preceding historical overview, generalizations can be made concerning the aesthetic and artistic development of electronic music for the Cunningham Dance Company, and the impact of this music on audiences, critics, the Cunningham dancers, and subsequent creative artists.

The Cunningham Dance Company musicians had access to the standardized, mass-produced electronic music equipment developed after 1965 (when the synthesizers of Robert Moog, Don Buchla, and others became commercially available). But except for specifically practical devices such as tape recorders, mixers and (from the 1980s) digital computers and sound-processing equipment, the Cunningham Dance Company musicians preferred the challenge, risk, and reward of electronic instrument building and system design. This resulted in non-standard, often one-of-a-kind systems unique to each piece. The impetus of the explorer prevailed.

In contrast to this explorer tendency was the predominant tide of homogeneity in electronic music culture elsewhere. The attraction of easy commercial and academic acceptance warped the aspirations of many musical artists, who succumbed to using electronic technology in the pursuit of imitating the sounds and musical culture of acoustical instruments, rather than exploring musical possibilities indigenous to electronic resources.

The idea of "product" was fundamental in that regressive cultural tide. The vision of its practitioners rarely extended beyond shallow entertainment possibilities for their work. For the Cunningham musicians the concept of "process," and the exploring of artistic risks remained a more attractive cultural goal.

The public – audiences and critics – and sometimes even the Cunningham dancers, were not always happy with the music. The music for *Winterbranch* (1964) received complaints about being too loud, but loudness was only one of several challenging aspects of the work. *Winterbranch* began with threateningly ambiguous silence; the visibility of the dancers was obstructed by unpredictable occurrences of total darkness. The initial ambiguous silence was followed by two abrasive sounds that continued relentlessly until the end of the dance. And because those two sounds did not develop in culturally familiar ways, audience preconceptions about what music was or should do were seriously challenged.

This was not the earliest such challenge in the Cunningham repertory – Cage's music for *Antic Meet* (1958) also generated controversy. But the vigorously loony wit of Cunningham's choreography distracted audience attention from challenges inherent in Cage's music for *Antic Meet*. Those challenges were fundamental to most of the music for the Cunningham Dance Company after 1960, beginning with this profoundly important matter: the dancers and musicians were not dependent upon each other. The Cunningham repertory established the principle of dancers not dancing to or being driven by music. In work after work, over the decades, Cunningham's modern dance masterpieces demonstrating this principle appeared in a steady accumulation.

More difficult than the (sometimes justified) complaints about loudness was dealing with Cunningham Dance Company music in the perspective of traditional musical aesthetics. Much of the Cunningham repertory did not use the sounds and gestures of traditional musical vocabulary. But unusual and innovative sound vocabulary preceded the use of electronics. Cage's prepared-piano music, and timbre-modified pianos in works such as *Suite for Five* (1956), were difficult for some of the public. The use of sounds previously considered "unmusical" was a challenge for some, though the post-World War II era was generally a time of rapid expansion of the musical sound vocabulary.

The structural characteristics of the music were often beyond those of traditional western art music. The Cunningham Dance Company music could be mobile or "open-form," and sometimes virtually formless. Some of the music seemed time-suspending, or was without the audience-reassuring devices of recognizable musical syntax. Cage's entirely verbal compositions, some composed using chance operations, could be completely asyntactical (as in his important late writing of the *Mesostics*, and *I-VI*, the 1989 Charles Eliot Norton Lectures at Harvard University). These music procedures resulted in substantial and sometimes radical departures from familiar aesthetic traditions, difficult confrontations of audience expectation, and challenges even to basic cognition.

Such departures from aesthetic tradition and audience expectation were certainly not special to Cunningham Dance Company music. The history of 20th Century music from Debussy, Schoenberg, and Stravinsky's *Le Sacre* onwards has been filled with such challenges. With repetition, public familiarity with that music has attenuated the challenges.

But much of the Cunningham repertory has music that is not fixed, not repeatable, thus precluding eventual, comforting familiarity. Some of this music varies in detail and structure from one performance to another but, like Tudor's *Rainforest*, maintains an identifiable and attractively accessible sound vocabulary. A different example is Oliveros's *In Memoriam Nicola Tesla*, which maintains a secure musical architecture in spite of an encompassing sound vocabulary that can seriously distract audience attention from the choreography.

It can be an insecure proposition to complain that the music should distract from the dance. Such distraction was an engaging feature of the on-stage reading by the champagne-sipping John Cage of his *Indeterminacy* stories, which collided sometimes recklessly with the ebullient choreography of Cunningham's celebrated *How to Pass, Kick, Fall, and Run* (1965).

Some of the variable or open-form music from the Cunningham repertory has become fixed – frozen and repeatable – by its release on commercial sound-recordings (and regretfully disembodied from the dance). Examples include the music for *Place* (1966), *RainForest* (1968), and *Five Stone Wind* (1988). Video recording and films have frozen – made repeatable – otherwise variable work. Examples include *Variations V* (1965), and *Channels/Inserts* (1981). But such fixing is an artifact of technology inadequate to do more than capture and repeat. It is at best a translation from a live medium to a canned medium; though perhaps better than nothing, canned is not fresh.

If cognition was occasionally a musical challenge, musical perception could also be difficult. Some composers made music that was the opposite of "too loud," that is, "too quiet," and explored issues of ambience and acoustical perception at the periphery of audibility and into inaudibility. At the threshold of audibility everyone hears something different; some hear nothing at all – a particularly interesting circumstance for aesthetic speculations about music.

Recent work and conclusion

Recent music for the Cunningham Dance Company continues in some directions established earlier, though often using more recent electronic technology. The digital computer has become an important resource. Large, mainframe computers have been used for composition and sound processing, as in the music for *Points in Space* (1986, John Cage's *Voiceless Essay*) in which the sounds of the composer's speaking voice were removed, leaving only Cage's unvoiced phonemes as the essential musical vocabulary. The glow of laptop portable computers is seen in the orchestra pit, where the musicians use them to control aspects of live performance. David Tudor explored the exotic world of neural networks – digital circuits that can be adventurously self-teaching and develop their own creative and musical responses.

Tudor's contribution as a composer with electronic resources has developed from the now-legendary *Rainforest* into a formidable repertory of pioneering works. After *Sounddance* (1975, Tudor's *Toneburst*), a new work employing a complex electronic system appeared at three-year intervals. These include *Exchange* (1978, Tudor's *Weatherings*), *Channels/Inserts* (1981, Tudor's *Phonemes*), *Phrases* (1984, Tudor's *Fragments*), *Shards* (1987, Tudor's *Webwork*), *Polarity* (1990, Tudor's *Virtual Focus*), and *Enter* (1993, Tudor's *Neural Network Plus*).

Composer collaborations still occur, manifestations of creative explorers on an electronic technology adventure and, as in the choreographic and musical epic

Five Stone Wind (1988, music by Cage, Kosugi, and Tudor), continue to result in collective masterpieces.

An important attribute of the musical component of the Merce Cunningham Dance Company, with or without electronic music resources, is the pushing of the envelope of possibilities. This attribute sometimes causes consternation. But it is a wellspring of confidence and exuberance for creative artists, in all of the creative arts: music at extremes of loud and quiet, dance at extremes fast and slow, lighting at extremes of dazzle and dark, decor at extremes of sparse and cluttered. It is from the enormous range of possibilities between extremes of too much and too little that wonderful ideas flourish – and nourish the so often transcendent art of the Merce Cunningham milieu.

Choreography and Dance, 1997, Vol. 4(3), p. 59–78
Photocopying permitted by license only

Merce Cunningham and John Cage: Choreographic Cross-currents

William Fetterman

John Cage and Merce Cunningham, 1964. Photo: Hans Wild.

The over-fifty-year collaboration of John Cage and Merce Cunningham is typically known for the independence of the music and the dance, sharing only a common duration. However, Cage composed a movement score for the conductor's part in *Concert For Piano and Orchestra* (1957–58). Cunningham performed the conductor's part at the first performance in 1958.

This essay documents Cage's score and Cunningham's performance, with attention to choreographic notation. The conclusion is concerned with time theory, as exemplified in the work of both artists. Taken in context, Cage's score for the conductor in *Concert For Piano and Orchestra*, and Cunningham's performance, constitute a summation of their mature collaborative process between the music and the dance as separate yet mutually inclusive entities.

KEY WORDS   Choreography, conducting, liminality, music, notation, time

The long collaboration of Merce Cunningham (choreography) and John Cage (music) is one of the most significant developments in twentieth-century theatre. John Cage has defined theatre this way:

> I try to make definitions that won't exclude.
> I would simply say that theatre is something which engages both the eye and the ear. The two public senses are seeing and hearing; the senses of taste, touch, and odor are more proper to intimate, non-public situations. The reason I want to make my definition that simple is so one could view everyday life itself as theatre.
>
> (Kirby & Schechner 1965, 50)

Cage's own definition of theatre would become complete in his audial/visual compositions (beginning with *Water Music*, composed in the spring of 1952 for the pianist David Tudor), but it is in his work with Merce Cunningham that Cage has been most generally acknowledged in the theatre.

However, this minimizes the work of both individuals. The choreography and music, independently composed, share only a common time and place of performance. It is therefore most convenient and practical to view Cunningham's choreography and Cage's music as being separate, non-causal simultaneities. Discussing Cage's music of the last forty years, however, involves notation indeterminate of its performance; and discussing Cunningham's choreography involves the minute parameters of both concept and realization. One then talks of theatre, yet must discuss two very different phenomena. The problem with indeterminate musical notation is that no two performers or performances may have the same content or result. The traditional view of composition as a fixed sequence of events thus fails when one tries to analyze much of Cage's music. In dance, this becomes even more problematic, not only because there is, unlike in traditional music, no standard notation; but also because we are culturally not trained to observe dance. Even Cunningham has stated:

> Yes, it's difficult to talk about dance. It's not so much intangible as evanescent. I compare ideas on dance, and dance itself, to water... I'm not talking about the quality of the dance, but about its nature.
>
> (Cunningham & Lesschaeve 1985, 27)

Given this rather liminal (inbetwixt and inbetween) beginning, this essay will examine the Cunningham/Cage collaboration as a mutual influence, by looking at Cunningham's performance of the conductor in Cage's *Concert For Piano and*

Orchestra (1957–58), and the use of Cage's time-aesthetic in Cunningham's *Pictures* (1984).

Concert for Piano and Orchestra was first performed on 15 May 1958, at the 25-Year Retrospective Concert of the Music of John Cage at Town Hall, New York. This was recorded and appears in the three-record set of the entire event (Cage 1959). Some visual description appeared in the *New York Times* review, which noted that *Concert For Piano and Orchestra...*

> ...presented some of the craziest mixed-up sounds ever heard on a concert platform....
>
> Since the thirteen instrumentalists included two tuba players and a trombonist, as well as assorted players, some of the grunts and squeaks can be imagined. David Tudor, the pianist, was fiddling with dials to produce electronic sounds as often as he was at the keyboard. And he was plucking and punching the strings more often than he was striking the keys in the conventional way. Toward the end he jiggled a "slinky" up and down.... This particular performance, which was led by Merce Cunningham, took twenty-five minutes.
>
> (Parmenter 1958)

Virgil Thomson also noted a few additional visual details:

> With the same man playing two tubas at once, a trombone player using only his instrument's mouthpiece, a violinist sawing away across his knees, and the soloist David Tudor crawling around the floor and thumping his piano from below, for all the world like a 1905 motorist, the Town Hall spectacle, as you can imagine, was one of cartoon comedy.

While Thomson's review might seem to be patronizing, he also characterized the work as "humane, civilized, and sumptuous" (Thomson 1960).

The score for *Concert For Piano and Orchestra* consists of separate score parts, complete within themselves. The piano part is 63 pages, with 84 different types of notation. The orchestra parts are solos for three violins, two violas, violincello, bass, flute, clarinet, bassoon (or baritone saxophone), trumpet, trombone, and tuba. Each orchestra solo is 16 pages, with five conventional five-line staffs per page. Each page of the piano part and a single staff in the orchestral solos is termed a "system" through which the performer determines time horizontally for the conventionally (i.e. vertically) notated tones. Note-heads are not employed for occurrence or duration. Cage's directive is that...

> ... the time-length of each system is free. Given a total performance time-length, the player must make a program that will fit it. The action of the conductor (when there is one) will alter the length of minutes (time-units). Therefore, in the circumstances of having a conductor, the player's program should be made so that he will be able to play faster or slower than he would with a standard chronometer.
>
> (Cage 1957–58)

The piano solo, written for and performed by David Tudor, is one of Cage's most imaginative compositions. Although it is a piano composition, Tudor fully exploited the score, using the keyboard, the inside of the piano, the body of the instrument, and auxiliary sounds such as blowing whistles or making electronic sounds. In performance, Tudor was no doubt very interesting to observe on the purely visual level.

The conductor's score is not, like a conventional music score, a complete notation that includes all the solo instrumental parts. Rather, it is a separate solo unto itself, a solo among other solos. The conductor's score notates arm movements through clock time as a physical representation of an analog (i.e. "circular") clockface. For Cage, the purpose of writing the conductor's score as an independent entity was:

> Giving up control so that sounds can be sounds (they are not men [i.e. sounds are not Beethoven]: they are sounds) means for instance: the conductor of an orchestra is no longer a policeman. Simply an indicator of time – not in beats – like a chronometer. He has his own part. Actually he is not necessary if all the players have some other way of knowing what time it is and how that time is changing.
>
> (Cage 1961, 72)

(The punctuation, including the bracket, is by Cage).

The choice of Merce Cunningham, a dancer and choreographer, to give the first performance as the conductor of *Concert For Piano and Orchestra* was probably motivated by several factors. On the most practical level, Cage and Cunningham had known and collaborated with each other already for several years. Cage would recently reply that he chose Cunningham because "he was available. I knew he could do it" (Cage 1986). Cunningham is, apart from being a very poetic and dramatic dancer and choreographer, also very musical in his work. To state that Cunningham is musical is not merely a metaphor, but an historical fact. He was an occasional musician in various concerts for Cage's percussion ensemble in the late 1930s and early 1940s. For instance, Cunningham is listed as a musician at a concert on 19 May 1939 (when both were still at the Cornish School in Seattle) (Program 1939), and is pictured in the Life magazine photo-essay as a musician in the Museum of Modern Art percussion concert of 7 February 1943 (*Life* 1943). Of the beginning of their mature collaboration in the mid-1940s, Cunningham would later state:

> My work with John had convinced me that it was possible, even necessary, for the dance to stand on its own legs rather than on the music, and also that the two arts could exist together using the same amount of time, one of the eye and the kinesthetic sense, the other for the ear.
>
> (Cunningham & Lesschaeve 1985, 141)

A reproduction of the first of two pages from the conductor's score for *Concert For Piano and Orchestra* appears in Figure 1. The way of reading the score may be further clarified. Not included in the original written instruction is how to use the "omit" time" column. Cage recently explained that this is subtracted from the clock time column, but only at the horizontal line on which one begins (Cage 1986). Beginning at the first line, only 30″ is omitted within a performance; the 15″ from the second line would thus be disregarded. At other lines there is 00″ to be omitted. In line eight is a different circumstance. 1′30″ is to be omitted from a clock time of 30″. If starting the performance on line eight, the performer would

CONDUCTOR

Using a stop-watch, the conductor changes clock-time to effective time. Standing where he may be seen by all the players, he represents to them the movement of a second-hand, but counter-clockwise (beginning each minute with the left arm high and descending to the left. At effective 30" the right arm continues to the right and up to effective 60". When a change in speed is approaching he indicates this with his free hand, an upwards motion announcing a faster speed, a descending one announcing a slower one. Throughout the final minute he keeps the free arm at 0, the end being indicated by the touching of the two palms.

He may begin anywhere in the following table, provided clock and effective time are accompanied with an omission number (in this case provided for a twenty minute program), continuing sequentially.

CLOCK TIME	EFFECTIVE TIME	OMIT	CLOCK TIME	EFFECTIVE TIME	OMIT
1'30"	15"	30"	30"	45"	00 "
1'30"	1'30"	15"	2'00"	1'15"	00"
1'15"	2'00"	00"	1'15"	1'15"	15"
1'15"	1'45"	00"	1'30"	30"	
30"	30"	15"	30"	30"	
1'30"	15"	15"	30"	15"	
15"	15"	00"	1'45"	45"	
30"	45"	1'30"	30"	45"	
15"	15"	45"	1'30"	30"	
45"	1'30"	30"	1'45"	45"	
1'15"	1'45"	00"	15"	30"	
1'15"	1'30"	00"	1'15"	1'45"	
1'30"	15"	00"	1'00"	1'00"	
1'45"	15"	00"	1'15"	45"	
1'45"	30"	30"	1'15"	1'00"	
2'00"	15"	00"	45"	1'30"	
1'00"	15"	00"	15"	15"	
1'30"	1'45"	15"	30"	45"	
30"	15"	00"	2'00"	15"	
1'00"	1'00"	00"	45"	30"	
15"	30"	15"	2'00"	45"	
1'15"	1'15"	1'15"	30"	30"	

Figure 1 The first page of the conductor's score in John Cage's *Concert For Piano and Orchestra* (1957–58).

have to divide the omission time into smaller units, which then would be sub-tracted from the next successive lines. Again, if starting on line 22, the clock and omission times are both 1'15", in effect cancelling the line entirely, or resulting in 1'15" of silence. As the conductor may begin on any line and end on any line, the total duration of performance is open. Conceivably it could take only a few min-utes. Were one to interpret the score as circular, it could continue for several hours or for infinity. If one does not interpret the score as potentially circular, but begins at the first line and goes through the entire score, the total clock time is 55'00". Correcting this total with the omission of 30", the complete score is 54'30" clock time. Once having determined the total duration of the performance, the conduc-tor uses his arms according to the "effective time" column to denote a faster or slower tempo of playing by the instrumental soloists.

Cunningham has recently recalled his performance:

> John asked me to do it because he thought it was physically difficult. In a way it is, but it soon doesn't become difficult.

> I recall my arms being very tired, because you had to hold your arms up, and this is to indicate fifteen, thirty, forty-five, and a minute; and if you go very slow, the players make few sounds, or if the arms move fast, they play faster. It's not so much about slow or fast as more sounds or less sounds.

> [Question: Was there much rehearsal?]
> Not with the orchestra, but I did by myself to learn how to do that, because you had to watch the watch, and sort of keep track of your score – not for the musicians, but for yourself – and since it was the first time it had been done, it was sort of strange (laughs).

> In the beginning it was hard to do. Later I learned to do it, but in the begin-ning it was, because it was new. It's not difficult once you get the idea, it's just the first time it's strange, and it was curious for the players to get used to this idea of seeing that that way. It's like looking at a clock, of course, but you soon get over that.
> (Cunningham 1989)

In the Town Hall recording, the performance has a duration of approximately 23'40". Looking at the score, one can reconstruct what Cunningham used on that specific occasion. The first 22 horizontal lines add up to a clock time of 24'15" which, when corrected with the omission of 30", gives a total clock time duration of 23'45". Clearly, Cunningham performed the score with extreme fidelity and precision.

The only other available documentation of Cunningham's performance is a still photograph (in Kostelanetz 1974, illustration 31). The angle from which the photograph was taken is from the audience, in a front row at the left of the audi-torium. It is difficult to tell exactly where Cunningham is within Cage's score. The right arm appears to be almost at a position of effective time 45" (or 270°), but the left arm is also extended in a curve, with the palm turned inward. Clearly at this point the left arm is being used to indicate to the musicians a change in arm movement speed, which correspondingly means that either an increase or decrease of tempo is to occur. This is the situation that is in Cage's score between lines 6 and 7; 8 and 9; 10 and 11; 12 and 13; 15 and 16; and 21 and 22. Going from lines 6 to

7, there is an increase in tempo. All the other examples noted here mark a decrease in tempo. From the position of Cunningham's left hand in the photograph, it is quite possible that he was at one of the points where tempo is to change from faster to slower.

Cage's score is choreography in the most literal and historical definition of the term. "Choreography" commonly means that someone (a "choreographer") makes up a dance, and teaches it to the other performers. Literally, however, "choreography" means a written, notated dance (or by extension, composition of human movement), which the dancer or dancers then learn from reading a score. The term was first used by Raoul Auger Feuillet in his book *Chorégraphie, ou l'Art de Décrire la Danse* published in 1700 (Guest 1984, 63). The purpose of notated dance was to "improve the level of dancing, and to establish sound theoretical principles for the art" (Hilton 1981, 45). There have been many attempts at creating a standard dance/movement notation since the eighteenth century. In the twentieth century there have been several systems, most notably Laban and Benesh notation. The interested reader should refer to Ann Hutchinson Guest's 1984 book *Dance Notation* for further information and analysis. However, Guest decries the still-prevalent ignorance that there is no such thing as systematic movement notation, and the fact that contemporary dancers and "choreographers" do not regularly study and learn dance notation systems as a necessary part of their education. Analogous to this would be musicians who do not learn music notation, but learn to play their parts by imitating what the "composer" shows them to do; or actors who cannot read written language, but have to learn their parts orally from the "playwright."

Cunningham's own written notes for his own dance compositions are in personal shorthand, too abstract or incomplete to reconstruct the dance that he himself dances or teaches. He has written:

Notation [:] all of these systems based as they are on symbols which are translated by the dancer, are out of whack. The element of them that always troubled me was the translating act. The notator looks at a step, translates it into a symbol, writes it down, then at some time later, the dancer looks at a symbol, translates back into a step, and then does it.

But this is not the way a dancer acts. In his class and in his rehearsing, he looks directly at a step, or someone doing a movement, and reorganizes that immediately into his own body. It is more direct than the symbol syndrome....
I feel the symbol notation is an unnecessary hang-up with the past frame.
(Cunningham 1968, n.p.)

What is significant, however, is that as an orchestra conductor, Cunningham had to learn his movements not from literally imitating another dancer, but from reading a score; and that Cage, as a true choreographer (movement-notator), did not rely upon previous systems of dance notation, but invented his own, and very practical, system.

For the eye to visualize the movements more clearly that Cunningham would have performed in using the first 22 lines from Cage's score, the following three pages of Figure 2 are a renotation into the pictographic dance notation of Friedrich Zorn. Although the Laban or Benesh notation systems are historically contemporary with Cage's composition, Zorn's late-nineteenth century system is used for

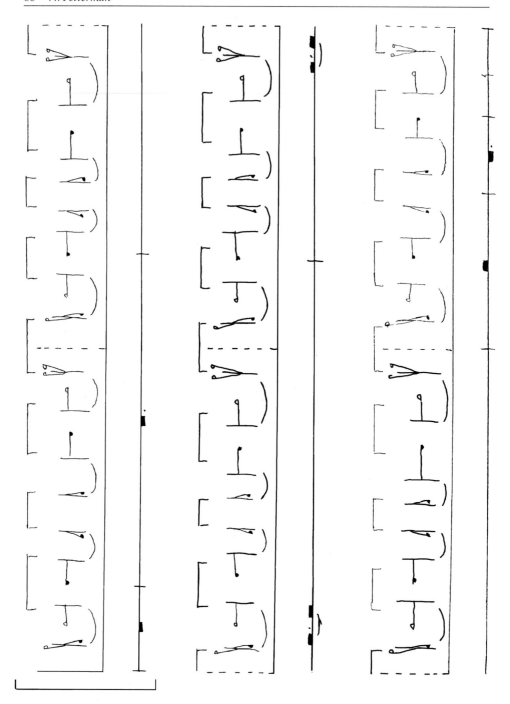

Figure 2   John Cages's first 22 lines in the conductor's score for *Concert For Piano and Orchestra*, renotated into the dance notation of Friedrich Zorn.

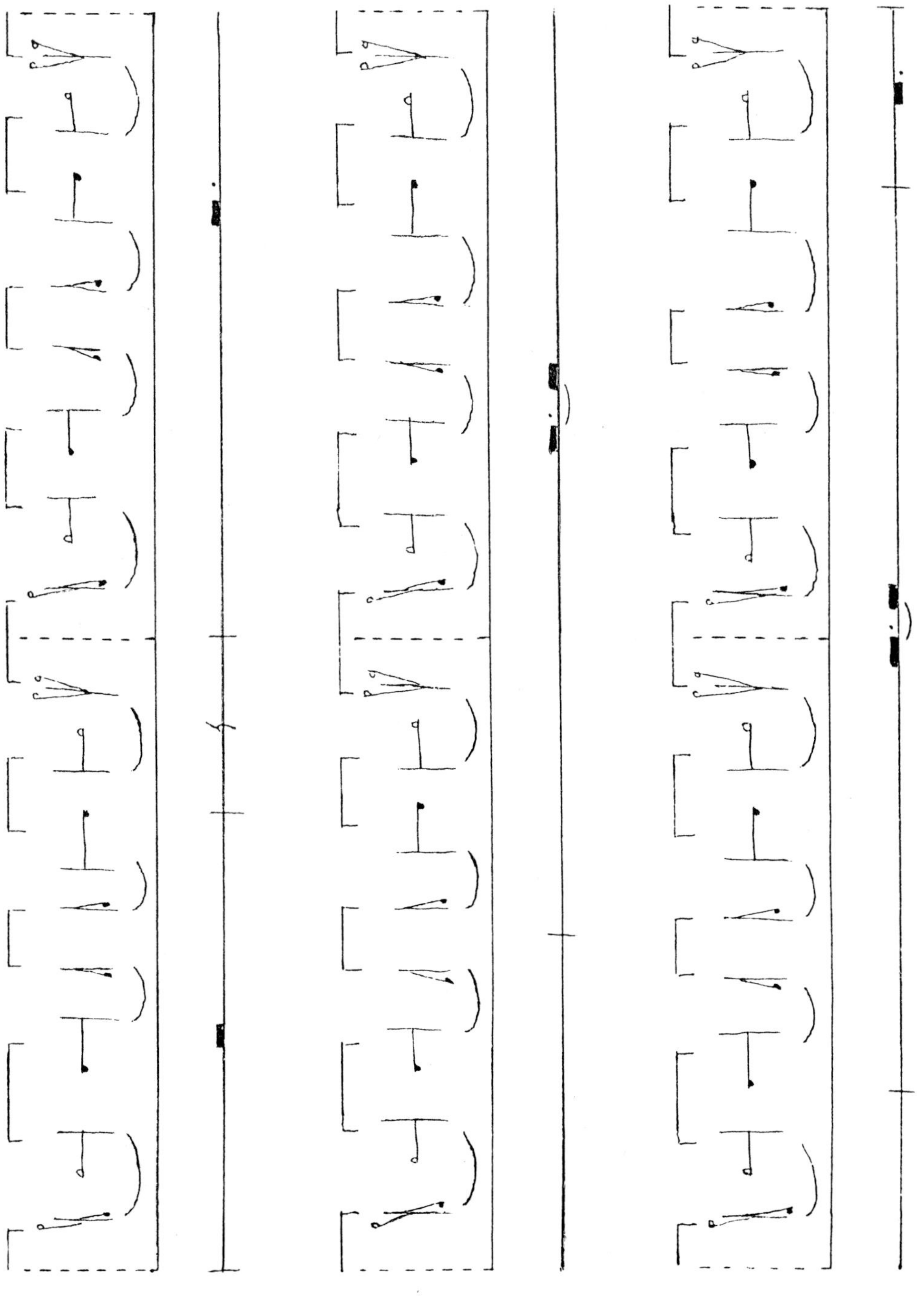

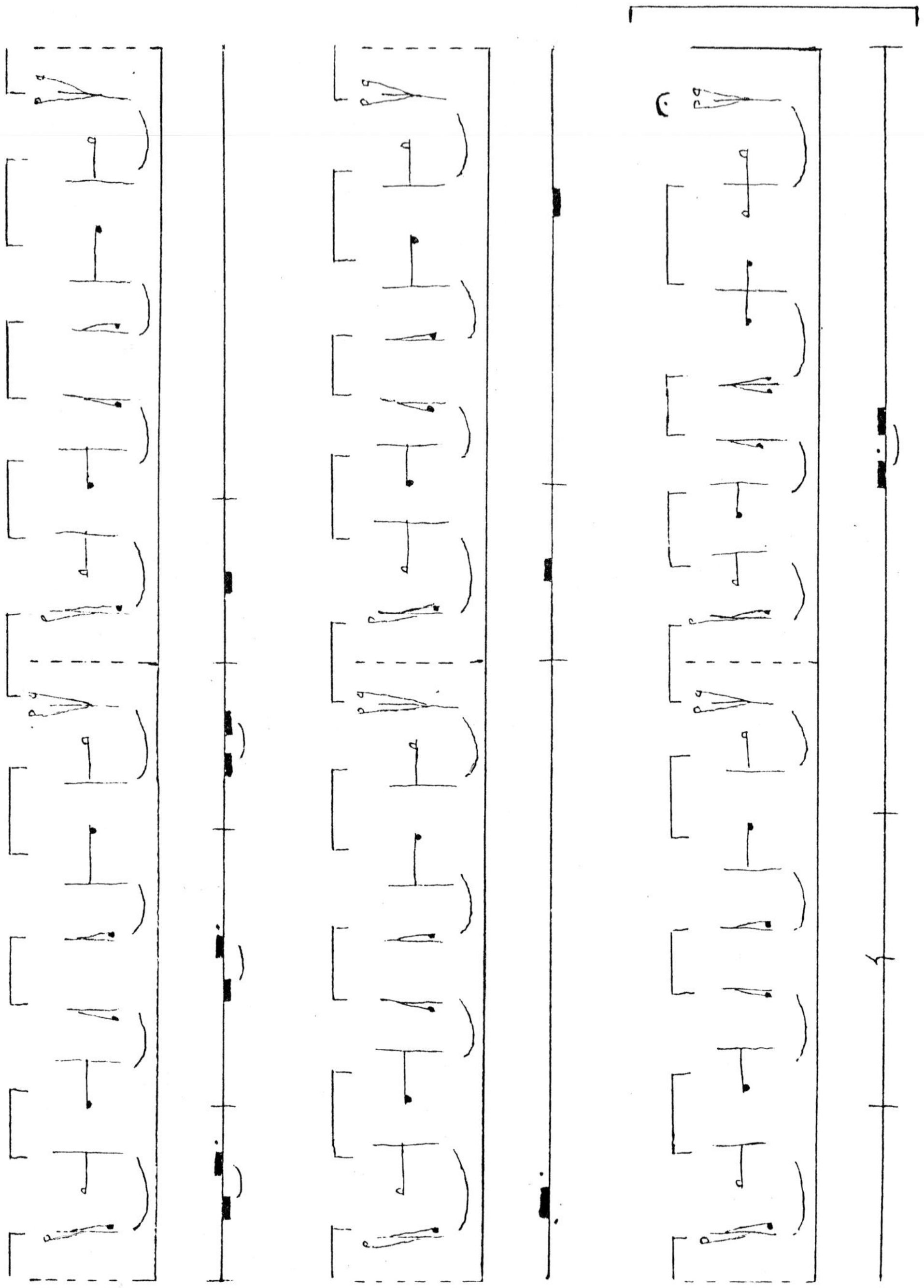

several practical reasons. Movement notation is rarely used systematically in "choreography." As a society we are still illiterate in movement notation (and, indeed, many in contemporary society are ignorant of music notation). The choice of a now-obsolete dance notation underscores this fact. However, instead of the more abstract system of Laban, or the shorthand stick-figures of Benesh, the more complete and representational stick-figures of Zorn allow for greater reading comprehension. Also, since Cage's choreography is to be representational of a clock face in actual performance, Zorn's system is not only convenient and practical, but organic as well (Zorn 1905).

In Figure 2, the left side of each figure corresponds to the performer's left side. Only the upper torso and arms are notated. An open circle means the palm is turned up to the ceiling; a closed circle means the palm is turned down to the floor. Movement through arm positions is notated with a tie-sign below the figures, as with tones in conventional music notation. The time within which movement is performed is notated on a time-line below the movement staff, retranscribed into traditional music symbols. A quarter-rest is equal to a metronome marking of 15 M.M., or fifteen seconds. Square brackets above the figures refer to either the turning of the palm, or the changing from one arm to the other. Not included in this renotation is the use of the free arm, as specified in Cage's score for showing a change in arm speed.

While this pictographic re-notation is only a synthetic reconstruction, it still gives the eye an approximation of Cunningham's actual movements according to the original score. Comparison between Cage's original and the renotated version also reveals minor but significant differences. Starting with the first line, the 30" is omitted during the first clock time of 1'30", making this 1'00". The effective time (the area of arm movement) is 15". In renotating, the 30" is also omitted from the effective time in the second line, making this 1'00". Omitting 30" from the effective time results, in this example, in having the arms end at 60" (although it must be noted that Cage does not suggesting using the omit column for the effective time as well).

The renotated version also incorporated two refinements that were physically demonstrated by Cage during an interview in 1986. Cage turns the palms when the left arm is at 15" or the right arm is at 45". This does not appear in the written score. Possibly Cage was teaching a refinement of interpretation which Cunningham had introduced in his actual performance. Turning the palms is what dancers do conventionaly when they raise or lower their arms to the side. The second refinement, which in Cage's teaching may again be the result of Cunningham's performance, occurs during the final minute. The written score stages that "throughout the final minute he keeps the free arm at 0, the end being indicated by the touching of the two palms." Instead, the renotated version has the two arms moving towards each other during the concluding effective time of 30", which is the manner that Cage demonstrated. Visually, this seems to be more effective than using only one arm, and a certain tranquility and finality is thus expressed in this manner. Otherwise, if one was following the original score, the left arm, having completed its movements, would have to be again immediately extended over the head at 0 for the right arm to touch it. As a result, the original score does not have the smooth and uninterrupted movement which occurs in Cage's later teaching (Cage 1986).

The tranquility of the final moments in *Concert For Piano and Orchestra* is just one example of Cunningham's variant dramatic endings to a dance. In the recording, the sound of the musicians is a rather dense wall-of-sound (one wonders whether the musicians were actually changing their tempos according to Cunningham's movements). Through all of this sonic chaos, Cunningham remained a center of quiet, disciplined focus, and the final touching of the two palms was a seminal gesture of his integral gracefulness. In his own choreographic works, Cunningham has made similarly organic "final gestures." In the 1966 film of *Variations V* (1965), he rides a bicycle wired for sound, around various electronic poles that also produce music (Árnbom 1966). In the midst of this complex technology, Cunningham concludes his otherwise rather austere dance work by riding the bicycle with the glee of a little boy exploring a birthday present. Again, in the complex video piece *Blue Studio*, there are many Merces dancing in multiple-exposure counterpoint. At the conclusion, the solo Cunningham makes a small gesture (akin to American baseball umpires when signaling "safe at base") to provide a simple coda to the previous complex events (Cunningham & Atlas 1975).

In terms of movement, one does not have to be a dancer or necessarily have any dance training to perform the role of conductor in *Concert For Piano and Orchestra*; however, it does not involve the conventional movements of a trained music conductor (i.e. beating time, giving entrance cues, and making emotional gestures and facial expressions to aid the musicians). Cage's choice of a dancer, rather than a musician, thus was a practical solution, for a dancer would not have the ingrained conventional habits of traditional practice to overcome. Michael Kirby succinctly defines "dance," apart from "everyday movement," as being "smooth muscle flow and complete muscular attentiveness" (Kirby 1978, 161). While there may seem to be little movement in the conductor's part, this score completely fulfills Kirby's abstract definition of dance.

Cunningham's own words about his dance technique provide further clarification concerning the practice and discipline of movement required:

> I thought that in modern dance, they used the torso, the back a great deal, the legs not so much. In the ballet, on the other hand, they used the legs a great deal, the arms too, in the great Russian school, and the back not so much, though the back obviously sustains the legs and arms. That's very general, but I wondered if there were some ways to put them together.... So my class usually starts with things for the back... it's the whole back actually that is at work. It affects the lower back because you don't let the hips go. Mostly when you bend over you let the hips go in order to counterbalance. I thought to try simply letting the legs go. You use the spine and pull the muscles in the back which people rarely use. That's why everybody has back trouble.

> It's because the arms are easy to move... one doesn't know how to hold them... And you have to learn to anchor the hips somehow. If you're not balanced in any position, whatever position you're in has no tranquility.

> All my work comes from the trunk, from the waist, nearest the hip, and you tilt it or you twist it in every direction. It doesn't come from the shoulders, but from much "r down.

(Cunningham & Lesschaeve 1985, 59–61).

Not everyone, however, has the physical strength or stamina to perform such a seemingly simple task. The balance, the need to work from the lower back, is very quickly felt when practicing the conductor's score for only a few minutes. Although Cage's score may not seem to do so, it requires the use of the entire body, just as sitting, standing, or walking also involve the entire body.

The cross-current between Cage's music composition, and Cunningham's own choreographic works, such as *Pictures* (1984), is in a "constellation time model," based on the image of a constellation of stars. Let the reader bear with me. Time appears to be a mystery to us, perhaps because it is so vast that we cannot truly understand it, much like the situation of a flea viewing a painting ten miles by ten miles square. Or again, perhaps time is so simple that we do not truly recognize it because of the very obviousness. Like the Sophist, once we have discovered a more real reality, we find it changes again, and we are still empty, lacking the whole truth. Likewise, in Zen Buddhism and Taoism it is recognized that at best man can become open to true reality only by being in harmony with the continually changing process of our existence (or, to rephrase this, to recognize time not as a noun but a verb, and to recognize further that language ultimately distorts the ultimate essence of reality). Therefore I propose a geometric model of time, with some trepidation. I do not assert that this accurately reflects either Cage's or Cunningham's intentions, but only provide some suggestions.

Before discussing the constellation, first let me review three other geometric evaluations of time – the circle, the line, and the dotted-line. Circular time may be observed in the cycle of seasons or the movements or starts and planets in the sky. This periodicity of external recurrence is found in both Plato's dialogue *Timaeus* and James Joyce's novel *Finnegans Wake*, which exemplify the conception that ultimately there is no beginning and no end, that our life-span is merely an external middle within a portion of a vast recurring cosmic cycle. The genesis of repetition is also thus found within the circular continuum. (The only explicit example of circular time in the work of Cage and Cunningham is in their 1947 ballet *The Seasons*.)

Time is understood as linear in both Aristotle's *Poetics* and within the Judeo/Christian tradition. Time has a definite beginning, a middle, and an end. The *Bible* is purposefully structured with the first book being *Genesis*, which deals with the creation; and the last book, *Revelation*, which deals with the end of time. Time is also cumulative – actual time began before man's creation, but at the end of time all humanity from the first to the last man will be judged before God. Our existence in this middleness is a cause of anxiety, for only God and not man is able to know the totality of time. In Matthew 25: 32–37 Jesus says:

> Now learn a parable of the fig tree; When his branch is yet tender, and putteth forth leaves, ye know that summer is nigh:
> So likewise ye, when ye shall see all these things, know that it is near, even at the doors.
> Verily I say unto you, This generation shall not pass, till all these things be fulfilled.
> Heaven and earth shall pass away, but my words shall not pass away.
> But of that day and hour knoweth no *man*, no, not the angels of heaven, but my Father only.
> But as the days of *Noe* were, so shall also the coming of the Son of man be.

(Another model of time, combing the circle and the line into a spiral, is likewise possible. The concept of the four seasons through succeeding years, where there is both sameness and repetition combined with change and the uniqueness of the actual moment, is logical, but perhaps only that.)

The third model of time as a dotted-line is the Christian Gnostic conception of time (see Puech 1957, 38–84). Man is inherently evil, and our understanding of time within a logical framework (the line, the circle, or the spiral) is false. Yet, God may grant man a glimpse of the truth, as in the empty space in between the segments of a dotted-line. This may be exemplified through another of Jesus's parables from Matthew 13: 31–32:

> Another parable put he forth unto them, saying, The kingdom of heaven is like a mustard seed, which a man took, and sewed in his fields:
> Which indeed is the least of all seeds: but when it is grown, it is the greatest among herbs, and becometh a tree, so that the birds of the air come and lodge in the branches thereof.

The dotted-line model of time is further supported in Victor Turner's concept of "liminality," that which is "in-betwixt and in-between," a state outside the ordered perception of time through which one receives inspiration, and from which one creates (Turner 1982, 20–59). It is the blank spaces in the dotted-line model that are most significant. This is not to be confused with being in an "outside time," rather the blank spaces reveal the more fully informed understanding of this cosmic mystery. In this model, too, it is a dotted-line because within our existence, sometimes we are experiencing lesser human time (the line), and sometimes we experience the more actual time (the blank spaces outside of the line).

The constellation model of time, which I believe Merce Cunningham's *Pictures* illustrates, derives from my reading of the *I Ching* with reference to John Cage's composition and thought. From the continual flux of yin and yang (broken and unbroken) lines changing into each other comes the evolution of the 64 hexagrams (six-line figures) of the *I Ching* (1967). The individual hexagram is not a static point in existence, but is merely a symbolic and transitory event which ultimately will change into another hexagram, a different event. When casting coins to determine a series of hexagrams through chance procedures, one notices that the progression is not "regular," it does not represent a seemingly logical succession of preconceived events. With the *I Ching*, one does not count numbers as 1, 2, 3, 4, etc.; one counts numbers more in the manner of saying 35, 3, 17, 41, etc. The chain of a cause-and-effect relationship thus becomes disjointed.

John Cage and Merce Cunningham have used the chance procedures and philosophy of the *I Ching* for the composition of music and dance since the early 1950s. The *I Ching*, together with aesthetics from Zen, has commonly shaped their long-continuing collaboration. Of this common thread, Cage has said:

> What Suzuki taught me is that we really never stop establishing a means of measurement outside of the life of things, and that next we strive to resituate each thing within the framework of that measure. We attempt to posit relationships between things by using this framework. So, we lose things, we forget them, or we disfigure them. Zen teaches us that we are in reality in a situation of decentering in relation to this framework. In this situation each thing is at the center. Therefore, there is a plurality of centers, a multiplicity of centers. And they are all interpenetrating and, as Zen would add,

Figure 3   Notation K, excerpted from the piano solo in John Cage's *Concert For Piano and Orchestra.*

non-obstructing. Living for a thing is to be at the center. That entails interpenetration and non-obstruction.

(Cage & Charles 1981, 91)

These concepts of centering, interpenetration, and non-obstruction resulted in
Cage beginning the idea of the "universe" or "constellation" in music notation
and performance in the mid-1950s. In *Winter Music* (1957), for example, the staffs
appear as isolated tonal events within a background of silence, of blank spaces,
reminiscent of stars in the sky (Cage 1957).

The piano solo in *Concert For Piano and Orchestra* provides two variant experimental notations which further extend this idea. In notation K (an example repro-
duced in Figure 3), the player is to:

Disregard time. Play only odd or even number of tones in a performance,
using others of a given 3, 4, 5, or 6 sided figure as graces or punctuations.

(Cage 1957–58)

In this example, there are two each of three, four, five, and six-sided figures. The notation is determinate in the actual tones to be played, but it is indeterminate with the occurrence and duration. It is possible to play only the odd- or even-sided figures as the primary tonal events (with then the even- or odd-sided figures as graces), but there is no determination with which figure or figures to begin or end with, nor is there any indication for which tone to begin with, or if one will read the figures clockwise or counterclock-wise. If one strictly adheres to Cage's instruction to "disregard time," the performer may use his final determined order of tones within an improvisational time-frame; or, one might measure the lengths of the lines connecting tones, and determine occurrence in space equal to time (say, a quarter of an inch equal to a quarter of a second).

Notation AK, a variation of K, appears as an example in Figure 4. For this, Cage writes as instruction:

> Play any 1 note in each 'universe' according to the time and amplitude given.
>   (Cage 1957–58)

In this example time is read horizontally as the occurrence of an event in space. Notations K and AK are like an umbrella — K is closed, and AK is opened-up spatially. However, notation AK still has several indeterminacies. Cage explicitiy notates tonalities, but the final selection of tones and their occurence is to be determined by the performer. Dynamics are notated underneath the staves, but are spatially independent in their vertical arrangement with the tones. Again, as in K, one is left with starting points – in AK, this is the center of each "universe," with E below the bass staff and C-sharp in the treble staff - but the resultant performance will not necessarily be a replication of the notation as it originally appears. (The horizontal brackets of 0, 2, and 4, above the staves, are rather mysterious. Cage does not provide any indication of their use in the accompanying instructions.)

In both notations K and AK, Cage invents variant notations that are indeterminate of their performance. The result is that any two different performers will make different versions of these notations. Notation AK is an early type of "universe," which Cage would later term a "constellation." Cage would later elaborate on its concept:

> I can accept the relationship between a diversity of elements, as we do when we do when we look at the stars, discover a group of stars and baptize it 'The Big Bear.' Then I make an object out of it. I am no longer dealing with the entity itself, seen as having elements or separate parts, I have before me a fixed object which I may cause to vary precisely because I know in advance that I will find it identical to itself. From this point of view, I am practicing what Schoenberg said: variation is a form, an extreme case of repetition. But you can also see how it is possible for me to get out of this circle of variation and repetition. By returning to reality, to that particular entity, to that constellation which is not yet completely a constellation. It is not yet an object! I can quite easily perceive the thing that from one perspective forms a single object as a group of different and distinct things. What makes the constellation into an object is the relationship I impose on its components. But I can refrain from positing that relationship, I can consider the stars as separate

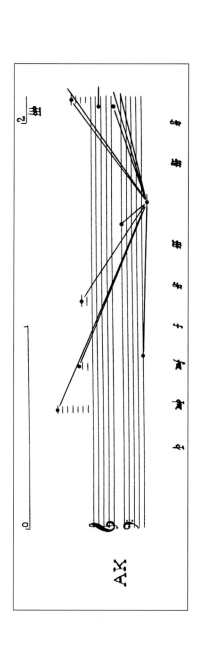

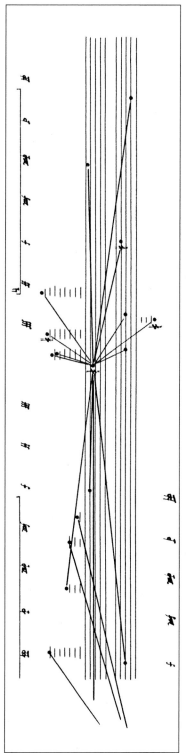

Figure 4 Notation AK, excerpted from the piano solo in John Cage's *Concert For Piano and Orchestra.*

yet close, *nearly* united in a single consellation. Then I simply have a group of stars.

(Cage & Charles 1981, 79)

It is the fault that music notation has not developed to be written and read three-dimensionally that becomes rectified in Merce Cunningham's choreography, most notably in *Pictures*. Cunningham's very practical use of time is centered within the dance itself, rather than taking the rhythms of music as movement cues (as in much other dance). This method of working independently of music, while still "sharing a common time" as a practical working-process to reveal the "continuing flexibility in relationship of the two arts [dance and music]" came about perhaps first in the extreme situation of dancing to concrete tape music in the early 1950s. Cunningham has said:

When you do not work to music or to a pulse to push you, you must in a sense push yourself, you must be your own horse rather than have something outside of you be the horse, you must find a way to sustain that, keep it going in the same sense. And you must be precise with yourself at the same time because you have freedom. I think perhaps one of the obvious things that conditions our work would be: we don't dance to a music, it does not push us; we really have to do it ourselves.

(Cunningham & Lesschaeve 1985, 30)

This method of working was illustrated when I observed a rehearsal directed by Mr. Cunningham of his company on the afternoon of 14 March 1986, at the City Center in New York City. When I arrived, most of the dancers were on stage, still limbering up, preparing for the formal rehearsal. Cunningham walked on stage, there was a bit of soft talking, then he went into the auditorium, sat down, announced softly which piece was to be run through, paused a few seconds, and then said "curtain [up]." The dancers went through each piece in turn. After each piece Cunningham would ask the company if they were satisfied or if anyone had a problem. What was extraordinary was that all through the dance rehearsal the musicians (David Tudor and Takehisa Kosugi) were checking the sound equipment, practicing short fragments from what they would perform later that evening, in general "warming-up." The music that was intermittently played (some of it unintentional mechanically) had nothing to do with the dance being rehearsed/performed at the moment. This did not detract from the dancers' perception of time, nor did this detract from my enjoyment of what was happening. Some part of David Tudor's extraordinary musicianship also becomes noticeable during rehearsal. For all of his reputation for noisy music performance, David Tudor uses his ears and his equipment in a remarkably cerebral, but also sensitive and emotional manner.

In part, one could enjoy the choreography of *Pictures* without the music – but some of the general appeal that *Pictures* enjoys is the very serene mood of the music (*Interspecies Smalltalk* by David Behrman) with its traditional-sounding harmonies and timbres. Cunningham has not found a larger audience, in part, because of his frequent use of music that 'bends the ears' (paraphrasing the composer Charles Ives).

In proposing the constellation model of time, I view the dance, apart from Behrman's music, as a three-dimensional representation of the process of change, as is reflected in the *I Ching* and in John Cage's music. The very term of "constellation" is used in Cage's sense of the word. On the most superficial level of visual comparison, the tableaux from *Pictures* seem to have much in common with the two previous examples of indeterminate piano notation. What dance can do more successfully is to reveal the more actual reality of events in space (though I am perhaps equating dance too closely with notation, treating dance as a living-notational form of time through movement). E.T. Kirby, writing on ancient masques, states:

> The hieroglyphic figures of the dance patterns also referred to an understanding of an original unity that was thought to have existed in earlier times before writing, music, acting, and other forms of expression became separated. The hieroglyph itself represents such a unity, for it combines many different meanings in a single, rather unwieldy and suggestive, pre-alphabetic symbol or emblem.
>
> (E.T. Kirby 1969, xv–xvi)

If we take Cunningham's tableaux to be hieroglyphs or hexagrams, one may see in the choreography a mature use of fluidity within the use of the stage-space and the individual as well as collective dancers' movements. Some tableaux are formed quickly and remain motionless for a longer or shorter duration, others only slowly evolve and are built-up or decreased with the addition or subtraction of individuals. In the formation and disintegration of a single tableau one may view the Zen aesthetic of interpenetration and non-obstruction. In a more complicated manner the stage-space itself may contain several tableaux at any one moment, each tableau forming and dissolving at a different tempo apart from the other tableaux. And yet these separate entities are not isolated from one another, but like one *I Ching* hexagram changing to another, a change and dissolving of one tableau is itself a beginning of a new tableau formation, a new event, a new unspeakable hieroglyph.

One aspect that makes *Pictures* so subtle and yet direct with thinking about time, is the element of stasis. Cunningham has said:

> My energy is nourished by motion. That is, thinking that even when one is still one is really in motion, so that one is constantly moving, one does not pose. I use this word specifically because it is a word I often heard at the [Paris] Opera: pose, and it conveyed a static quality to me. Even when we are still we are moving, we are not waiting for something, we are in action when we are still.
>
> (Cunningham & Lesschaeve 1985, 129)

Thus, in *Pictures* the tableaux may represent stasis, but do not reflect a stop-and-start view of time. What Cunningham expressed is the fluidity of time and change, on both an obvious and subtle level. When a picture is formed and remains in position for a duration, it is a gracious act through which one may recognize and meditate on the nature of time and existence as a constellation of multiple centers (within a single center), reflecting not the human tragedy of cause-and-effect, but the joy of being through the discipline of mindful process and attention.

Of course, it would be a mistake to believe that what I have written about *Pictures* and the *Concert For Piano and Orchestra* is at all what both Cage and Cunningham have intended, however purposefully purposeless their work may be. I enjoy the work of both artists because sometimes it wakes me up on the purely sensual level, sometimes it makes me think without necessarily being entertained, and sometimes it achieves all that and much more. Perhaps my understanding of *Concert For Piano and Orchestra* and *Pictures* is, through a synchronistic action, a part of what these works involve. Yet there is much more in both than I can either know or relate. If these two works are only a mimesis of time and not a truth, and if what I write is only a mimesis of a replication, I again ask the reader to bear with me, for in conclusion I ask the reader to let me yet smile, and apart from this essay, continue to enjoy and be nourished by the original mirror.

References

Arnbom, Arne (1966) *Variations V*, 50 min., black and white sound film of the Cage/Cunningham work. Hamburg: Nordeutscher Rundfunk. Available from the Merce Cunningham Foundation.

Cage, John (1957) *Winter Music*. New York: Henmar Press Inc.

———— (1957–58) *Concert For Piano and Orchestra*. New York: Henmar Press Inc.

———— (1959) *The 25-Year Retrospective Concert of the Music of John Cage*. New York: George Avakian. A three-record set with notes and score excerpts by the composer, recorded in performance at Town Hall, New York, 15 May 1958.

———— (1961) *Silence*. Middletown, Conn.: Wesleyan University Press.

———— (1986) Interview by author 9 April, New York.

Cage, John and Charles, Daniel (1981) *For the Birds*. Boston: Marion Boyars.

Cunningham, Merce (1986) *Changes*. New York: Something Else Press.

———— (1989) Interview by author 18 August, New York.

Cunningham, Merce and Atlas, Charles (1975) *Blue Studio: Five Segments*, 15 min., color video. New York: WNET/TV Lab. Available from the Merce Cunningham Foundation.

Cunningham, Merce and Lesschaeve, Jacqueline (1985) *The Dancer and the Dance*. New York: Marion Boyars.

Guest, Ann Hutchinson (1984) *Dance Notation: The Process of recording movement on paper*. New York: Dance Horizons.

Hilton, Wendy (1981) *Dance of Court & Theater: The French Noble Style, 1690–1723*. Princeton, N.J.: Princeton Book Company.

The I Ching, or Book of Changes (1967), translated by Cary F. Baynes from Richard Wilhelm's German translation from Chinese. Princeton, N.J.: Princetown University Press.

Kirby, E.T. (1969) Introduction. In *Total Theatre: A Critical Anthology*, edited by E.T. Kirby, pp. xiii–xxxi. New York: E.P. Dutton & Co., Inc.

Kirby, Michael (1978) An Analytical Approach to Post-Modern Dance In *Contemporary Dance*, edited by Anne Livet, pp. 156–167. New York: Abbeville Press.

Kirby, Michael and Schechner, Richard (1965) An Interview with John Cage. *Tulane Drama Review* Vol. 10, no. 2, pp. 50–72.

Kostelanetz, Richard, ed. (1974) *John Cage*. New York: Pelican Books.

Life (1943) Band bangs things to make music. 15 March, pp. 42; 44.

Parmenter, Ross (1958) Music: Experimeter (Zounds! Sounds by) John Cage at Town Hall. *The New York Times*, 16 May.

Peuch, Henri-Charles (1957) Gnosis and Time. In *Man and Time: Papers from the Eranos Yearbooks*, edited by Joseph Campbell, pp. 38–84. Princeton, N.J.: Princeton University Press.

Program (1939) for a performance by the Cage Percussion Orchestra at the Cornish School in Seattle, Washington. In the John Cage Archive, Northwestern University.

Thomson, Virgil (1960) John Cage Late and Early. *The Saturday Review* Vol. 43, January, pp. 38–39.

Turner, Victor (1982) *From Ritual to Theatre: The Human Seriousness of Play*. New York: Performing Arts Journal Publications.

Zorn, Friedrich A. (1905) *Grammar of the Art of Dancing*, edited by A.J. Sheafe. Boston: International Publishers.

Choreography and Dance, 1997, Vol. 4(3), p. 79–98
Photocopying permitted by license only

Merce Cunningham: Making Dances with the Computer

Thecla Schiphorst

Merce Cunningham has been using the computer choreographic software, LifeForms, to make new dances since December 1989. Over twenty years before LifeForms was installed in his Westbeth studio in New York City, Merce Cunningham wrote about the possibility of a computer technology that would enable three-dimensional figures to be displayed on a computer screen. His projects very closely describe features of the LifeForms computer choreographic system as it was designed and implemented twenty-one years later. Envisioned and developed as a creative tool for choreographers at the Computer Graphics and Multi-Media Research Lab at Simon Fraser University, LifeForms provides an interactive, graphical interface that enables a choreographer to sketch out movement ideas in space and time. While Cunningham's method of creating movement for dance has evolved and expanded as a result of working with LifeForms, the LifeForms system has also evolved in response to Cunningham's interaction and feedback. This paper describes Merce Cunningham's use of the computer choreographic software and development in dance, and from the point of view of Cunningham's own choreographic process. The author, Thecla Schiphorst is a member of the design team that created LifeForms, and has been working with Merce Cunningham in New York City since December 1989, supporting his creation of new dance with the computer.

KEY WORDS   Choreography, computers and dance, compositional process, LifeForms, dance history, Merce Cunningham

Introduction

"One can *make* things with it [LifeForms], one doesn't have to put things in one already knows...one can make discoveries, and that interested me from the beginning."

Merce Cunningham[1]

Merce Cunningham has been making new dance with the computer choreographic software LifeForms since December 1989[2]. During that time, Merce Cunningham has created eleven new dances with the assistance of LifeForms, a creative output which is prolific by any standard. Cunningham's capacity, not only to envision possibilities, but also to concretely materialize those possibilities through his work in dance, has raised public consciousness in a way that perhaps no other single figure in the world of dance or of computer technology could accomplish. It is clear from the outcome of Cunningham's work with LifeForms

---

[1]   Merce Cunningham quoted in the CNN television series: *Arts and Technology Report*, March 1991.

[2]   This collaboration between Merce Cunningham and Dr. Tom Calvert leading the LifeForms design team was brought about by two Italian producers, Natale Tulipani and Donatella Bertozzi early in 1989.

that the creative process of making dance has been enriched and expanded through the use of computer technology.

LifeForms was developed at Simon Fraser University at the Computer Graphics and Multi Media Research Lab under the direction of Dr. Thomas Calvert[3]. The author of this paper, Thecla Schiphorst is a member of the design team that designed and developed LifeForms, and has been working with and tutoring Merce Cunningham in New York City since December 1989, supporting his creation of new dance with the computer.

Merce Cunningham has commented on the computer's ability to re-define the imaginable, or even the possible. In an interview with Jennifer Dunning he said, "I have had the same fascination with movement that I've had all my life. I find it all just as maddening, mysterious and exhausting. The point is that dance need not refer to something else. It is what it is. But you can get fixed ideas, and it can get restrictive. So, I try to put myself in a precarious position."[4] Cunningham's work with LifeForms is an example of his propensity for the precarious position that discovery can provide. This paper describes Merce Cunningham's use of the computer choreographic software LifeForms, and places that work in a historical context both from the point of view of technological development in dance, and from the point of view of Cunningham's own choreographic process.

Merce Cunningham's Early Vision

Over twenty years ago in his book, *Changes: Notes on Choreography*[5], Merce Cunningham imagined the design of a computer system that would enable three-dimensional figures to be displayed on a computer screen. He spoke of these figures moving in spatial relationship to one another, thereby enabling a choreographer to visualize dance stored on the computer.

> I think a possible direction now [in 1968] would be to make an electronic notation... that is three dimensional... it can be stick figures or whatever, but they move in space so you can see the details of the dance; and you can stop it or slow it down... [it] would indicate where in space each person is, the shape of the movement, its timing.[6]

At the time Cunningham made this statement, computer technology to create or to display movement for three-dimensional human figures did not yet exist. Yet Cunningham's projections describe very closely features of the LifeForms

---

[3] See Calvert, T., Welman, C., Gaudet, S., Schiphorst, T., Lee., C., "Composition of Multiple Figure Sequences for Dance and Animation", Visual Computer (1991) 7: 114–121, Springer-Verlag, 1991, and Calvert, T.W., Bruderlin, A., Mah, S., Schiphorst, T., Welman, C., "The Evolution of an Interface for Choreographers", InterChi proceedings, InterChi Conference, Amsterdam, April 1993.

[4] Jennifer Dunning, quoting Merce Cunningham for "For Cunningham, Dance is as Mysterious As It Ever Was", *New York Times*, March 11, 1990.

[5] Merce Cunningham, *Changes: Notes on Choreography*, Something Else Press, Inc., New York, New York, 1968, edited by Frances Starr, unpaginated.

[6] Merce Cunningham, "From Notation to Video" *The Dancer and the Dance*, Marion Boyars Inc., 1980, pp. 188–189. In this excerpt Cunningham refers to his earlier statement about computers and notation that appears in *Changes: Notes on Choreography*, Edited by Frances Starr, Something Else Press, Inc. New York (1968).

computer choreographic system as it was designed and then used by him twenty-one years later.

> It seems clear that electronic technology has given us a new way to look. Dances can be made on computers, pictures can be punched out on them, why not a notation for dance that is immediately visual?[7]

Most notably, Cunningham's 1968 description, while listing many features that have since been incorporated into a system such as LifeForms, also describes areas of research which are still ongoing. For example, areas such as set and stage design, facial animation, and motion description that includes detailed representation of hands, fingers, and toes are research topics currently being explored. Cunningham remarks, most astutely, that although the technical issues are great, they are not necessarily greater than the cognitive constraints of our own imagination. He points out that in order to overcome these constraints we must allow ourselves to explore beyond our preconceptions of technology and find new ways of exploring the possibilities:

> I am aware there are problems [with] this. But assuming the technological arrangements could be facilitated, and given the pace of change why not this? ... then the only other difficulty is psychological.[8]

Perhaps most importantly, Cunningham foresaw that such a computer system could be used not only as a method of preserving dance, but also as a compositional system to create or to choreograph movement, and even entire dances:

> ... it is conceivable [that] one could choreograph with such a device. This appeals to me. More than the museum I like the actuality.[9]

Just as Merce Cunningham raised questions years before LifeForms was developed, researchers and designers of computer systems for dance have been concerned about issues of creativity, representation, and mechanization in their exploration of the possibilities of using computer technology for dance:

> One can wonder about the accuracy of *expression* which will be possible. Can the *soul* of a dance be animated? Or is this too much to ask... this aspect could lead to interesting studies in body language and communication. Can the effort of a movement be computerized?... there is potential value in [computer systems] being developed in regard to dance... we must always remember that dancing is for people.[10]

From the technological perspective, researchers in the area of computer technology and dance have recognized that the knowledge of dance is distinct in experience and representation from the knowledge of computer systems. Designing computer systems for dance has provided many challenges in bridging these different methods of accessing knowledge.

---

[7] *Ibid.*

[8] *Ibid.*

[9] *Ibid.*

[10] Calvert, T.W., J. Landis and J. Chapman (1979). "Notation of Dance with Computer Assistance", *New Directions in Dance*, D.T. Taplin ed., Pergamon Press, Toronto, p. 175.

In perhaps no other application of computers is there such a disparity between the modes of thought of the users of the system designers. The
challenge to bridge this gulf is likely to benefit humanity as a whole...
Computers can be humanized. How to do this may become clear from trying
to 'dance' on a computer.[11]

Examples of this movement toward interdisciplinary collaboration are evident
in the design and development of LifeForms.

The LifeForms Software

LifeForms functions simply as a tool for the artist. The possibilities keep
changing and expanding, but results will always depend on the creator's
curiosity and resources.[12]

Merce Cunningham

LifeForms has been under development at Simon Fraser University since 1986[13].
Envisioned and developed as a creative tool for choreographers[14], it provides
an interactive, graphical interface that enables a choreographer to sketch out
movement ideas in space and time. Versions of LifeForms run on the Apple
Macintosh and the Silicon Graphics Indigo and Indy computers.

Figure 1   LifeForms Choreographic Software.

[11]   Herbison-Evans, D., "Dance, Video, Notation Computers", *Leonardo*, Vol. 21, No. 1, pp. 45–50,
1988.

[12]   Anne Pierce quoting Merce Cunningham in "Cunningham at the Computer", *Dance USA/Journal*,
Summer 1991, pp. 14–15.

[13]   LifeForms has been described in Calvert, T., Welman, C., Gaudet, S., Schiphorst, T., Lee, C., "Composition of Multiple Figure Sequences for Dance and Animation", *Visual Computer* 7: 114–121,
Springer-Verlag, 1991.

[14]   LifeForms has also received a great deal of interest from animators, directors, athletic coaches,
and motion planners, because it enables the user to create, edit, and store three-dimensional human
and character movement sequences.

Merce Cunningham has been using the Silicon Graphics version of LifeForms in New York City since December 1989. While Cunningham's method of creating movement for dance has evolved and expanded as a result of working with LifeForms, the LifeForms system has also evolved in response to Cunningham's interaction and feedback. An important underlying research goal that has informed the development of LifeForms is the study of the design or compositional process.[15] In the design of the LifeForms system, it has been observed that computer technology is as much affected by the articulation of dance knowledge as dance and choreography is affected by the articulation of technological knowledge.[16]

The development of a computer tool for the creation of dance provides several research challenges. For example, dance embodies a wide range of movement possibilities, and often requires great physical virtuosity that extends the limits of a human body's physical ability and training. Therefore, what is learned from a computer tool that is used to create dance can be generalized for other forms of human motion planning. Also, choreography is a compositional design task that requires a set of skills that have to do with creating, structuring, and forming. Building a computer interface which interacts with a choreographer's design skill set requires an understanding of the mental model of the choreographer's design process[17]. In dance, where the creative idea is a *movement* idea, the goal is to be able to visualize and create movement on the body model in an immediate and responsive way, so that the computer tool can become a 'visual idea generator'.

Evolving Versions of LifeForms

Since December 1989, three distinct versions of the LifeForms system have been installed on Merce Cunningham's Silicon Graphics computer. In the first version of LifeForms installed on Cunningham's computer, an SGI Personal Iris, dance composition was based on stances. In this early version, single stances or positions could be created, assigned to dances, and moved in space and time. This prototype forms the basis of the model that is currently implemented on the Apple Macintosh. Stances representing single movement positions are the movement primitive[18] for the compositional process. Menus in this version contain a collection of individual stances or shapes.

Merce Cunningham has created all of his dances since 1991 using the Sequence Editor version of LifeForms. Individual stances were replaced by entire sequences of movement, and the Body Editor was replaced by the Sequence Editor. In this next version, the choreographer works with a complete movement phrase as a primitive. This modification represented a major conceptual shift and enabled

---

[15] Herbert Simon has suggested that composition can be thought of as a design process and identifies elements that are common in all the disciplines in which design plays a part. See Simon, H.A., (1981). *The Sciences of the Artificial*, The MIT Press, Cambridge, Massachusetts, 1981.

[16] Calvert, T.W. Bruderlin, A., Mah, S., Schiphorst, T., Welman, C., "The Evolution of an Interface for Choreographers", *InterChi Proceedings*, InterChi Conference, Amsterdam, April 1993.

[17] Johnson-Laird, P.N., *Mental Models*, Harvard University Press, Cambridge, Massachusetts, 1983.

[18] A primitive represents the building block which other higher level conceptual chunks are based. A stance-based system means that the dance must be constructed by stringing together individual positions or shapes.

composition to occur on a higher level of abstraction. Cunningham said of this change from stances to sequences:

> What was like photographs is now like film, and what started out as work with positions has developed into work with phrases... it's remarkable, they keep adding things to it... it will enlarge it [dance]... the system now has multiple possibilities.[19]

While the incorporation of the Sequence Editor in version two addressed an evolution in compositional support, the addition of *inverse kinematics*[20] in version three[21] addressed a shift in the way in which movement could be defined on the body model. It enables a choreographer to position a series of related limbs by directly selecting and moving an end point (such as the hand) and affecting an entire chain of limbs (the whole arm and spine) as a result.

LifeForms Functional Description

In describing the essence of dance Merce Cunningham has said: "Dancing is movement in time and space: its possibilities are bound only by our imagination and our two legs." LifeForms maps this viewpoint of movement in time and space by providing three on-screen windows in which to create dance: 1) a window which allows the creation of **movement** sequences for a single dancer; this is called the 'sequence editor' window; 2) a 'spatial' window which allows groups of dancers to be arranged and edited in **space**; and 3) a 'timeline' window, which allows the dancers' movement sequences to be moved and edited in **time**. These three windows or views are interconnected. One can move flexibly between them using a simple interactive and intuitive interface that supports the hierarchical nature of composition by allowing movement between conceptual levels of abstraction. In LifeForms, movement sequences can be *keyframed*[22] by directly configuring a body interactively. The system's large library of predefined movement sequences provides a source of material that can be performed by multiple human figures[23]. These figures can be edited in space, or in time using a simple interactive and intuitive interface. Movement paths can be viewed, and the playback of the move-

---

[19]   Robert Graskovic, quoting Merce Cunningham in *Los Angeles Times*, May 15, 1991.

[20]   Inverse Kinematics is a method for positioning the human body model interactively on the screen. The choreographer highlights a chain of limb segments to be pulled into position. For example, if the end of the chain is the hand and the base of the chain is the lower back, the entire chain from the base of the lower back can be moved by pulling on the hand.

[21]   The third version of LifeForms was installed in Merce Cunningham's studio in August 1992. It still used the Sequence Editor, but added *Inverse Kinematics* as a method of limb positioning.

[22]   A keyframe is used by the computer to calculate and display intermediate frames in a movement sequence. LifeForms automatically creates smooth human motion between any two positions, or "keyframes", defined by the user. For instance, one keyframe might show a human figure with its arms held up in the air, while another shows the figure with its arms pointing straight down. The software supplies the "in-between" frames.

[23]   LifeForms enables the user to define and use skeletons other than the human body with the same ease and flexibility that allow choreographers to create dance. This feature can be used in character animation.

ment sequence is automatically interpolated[24] by the computer by smoothing the motion between the shapes created on the body. Included with LifeForms are libraries of sequences to provide a source of material that can performed by many figures simultaneously. Sound files can be selected, cued to "in" and "out" points, and played in synchronization with the dance sequences.

The Sequence Editor Window

A movement sequence is the design "building block" in the LifeForms system. In dance, movement sequences are also called "phrases" or "movement motifs". The underlying rationale in selecting a sequence as the building block, is that the user can develop design "chunks"[25] that enable creation to occur on a more conceptual

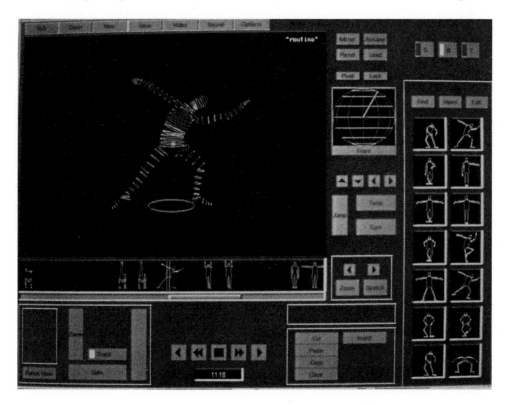

Figure 2   The Sequence Editor Window.

---

[24]   Interpolation is a mathematical function which estimates the missing value by taking a weighted average of known functional values at neighboring points.

[25]   Herbet Simon, in *The Sciences of the Artificial*, states that the capacity of short-term memory can be measured in terms of number of items or "chunks". This number has been shown to be between 4 and 7. The implication in computer user-interface design is that when the level of detail becomes too great (eg. > 7), the creative or design process is adversely affected because of the constraints of our short-term memory.

level. A sequence can be created, manipulated, varied, and placed together with other sequences. In LifeForms, the sequence editor is used to create a movement phrase for a single figure. A sequence is made up of a number of keyframes, each containing a body shape placed at user defined time intervals.

The Spatial View Window

The spatial view or 'stage', enables the choreographer to spatially plan multiple dancers performing combinations of sequences. A dancer can be assigned a sequence, a starting position, and an orientation (or "facing"), by directly positioning the dancer with the mouse. Movement can be viewed from any three-dimensional viewpoint, and camera keyframes can be set which enable the viewpoint to change as the composition is played back. These spatial scenes are similar to the series of story-board sketches used in planning film and video production, but the interactive capability allows the choreographer to zoom-in or zoom-out from the stage and to view the composition from all angles. The spatial view in conjunction with the timeline view allows spatial and temporal editing to occur in relation to one another.

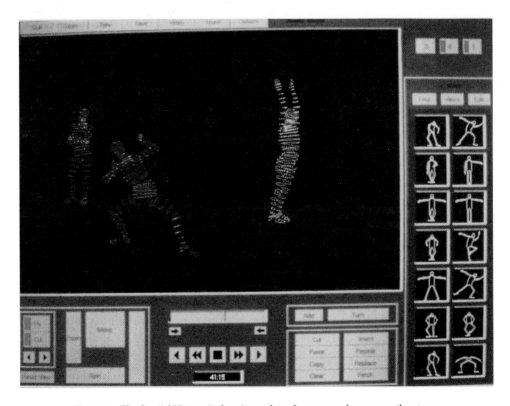

Figure 3   The Spatial View window is used to place many dancers on the stage.

The Timeline View Window

The timeline view provides the choreographer with a high-level score-like display that depicts the relationship between dancers and movement sequences. The spatial relationships of the dancers are superimposed upon the timeline display.

Since changes made to temporal relationship between figures and sequences necessarily result in changes to spatial relationships, the overlapping of views addresses this 'transparency' and interrelationship between space and time and provides immediate visual feedback when changes are made. Cunningham, speaking about the use of the spatial and timeline views, said: "I found composing dances on the computer to be marvelous. It suggests possibilities of time and space I've never thought of before."[26]

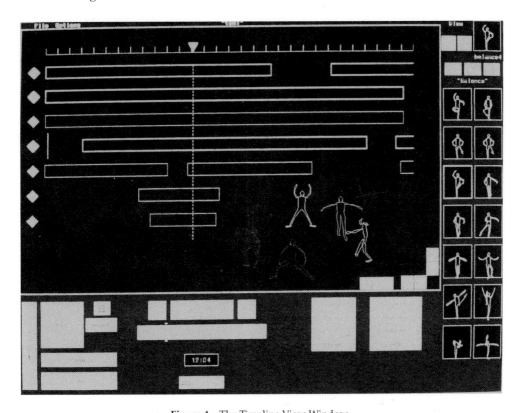

Figure 4 The Timeline View Window.

[26] Anne Pierce quoting Merce Cunningham in "Cunningham at the Computer", *Dance USA/Journal*, Summer 1991, pp. 14–15.

LifeForms Future Development

In addition to the work described above, experimentation has begun in connecting LifeForms to MIDI (musical instrument digital interface), to be projected and used interactively in live performance. Research is also underway to connect LifeForms to an interactive 3D input tracking system to enable movement to be sampled in real-time, and stored within LifeForms[27]. Other areas of research include facial animation, rendered bodies, articulated hand movement, and construction of stage sets.

Merce Cunningham's use of LifeForms

There is an enormous amount of choreographic and artistic knowledge that can enrich ways of using and creating with technology. Merce Cunningham has said, "I think of dance as a constant transformation of life itself."[28] It is not technological constraints that hold us back from using technology in new ways: technology changes at a tremendous rate. Our willingness to explore beyond the constraints of our imagination has the greatest effect on "the constant transformation". Merce Cunningham's work with dance and computer technology can be seen as an example. As Cunningham has said, "In looking for new movement I would look for something I didn't know about rather than something I did know about."[29] It is clear from the results of Cunningham's work with computer technology, that the design of LifeForms, and the design of the dances created with LifeForms can support that exploration and affect one another deeply.[30]

Examples of Merce Cunningham's work with LifeForms

In March, 1991, just over a year after he had been introduced to the LifeForms choreographic software, Merce Cunningham premiered a dance piece called *Trackers*, in which about one third of the movement was created with the computer. Cunningham said in a CNN interview, when talking about his use of LifeForms, "I think this technology can, in this case, particularly... open out a way of looking at dance and movement in a way that would be stimulating and invigorating to the whole dance field eventually."[31] Since that first computer-choreographed dance, Cunningham has continued to embrace technological possibilities as an extension

---

[27]   Thecla Schiphorst, "StillDancing: Interacting Inside the Dance", CHI 94, Interactive Experience Proceedings, CHI Boston 1994. This work has been supported by the Media Arts Section of the Canada Council.

[28]   Cunningham, Merce (1985) *The Dancer and the Dance: conversations with Jacqueline Lesschaeve*, Marion Boyars Publishers, New York, London, 1985, p. 27.

[29]   *Ibid*.

[30]   Calvert, T.W., Bruderlin, A., Mah, S., Schiphorst, T., Welman, C., "The Evolution of an Interface for Choreographers" *InterChi Proceedings*, InterChi Conference, Amsterdam, April 1993.

[31]   *Ibid*.

of his exploration of movement as a process, rather than as a fixed goal. He has created eleven dances which incorporate movement created in LifeForms, including *Beach Birds*, *CRWDSPCR*, *Enter*, and *Ocean*. Cunningham does not find it surprising that his references in dance are mirrored by references seen in technology, and in other art forms such as literature. He has responded to these comparisons to multiple references, images, and symbols, by noting that a relationship exists between the development of artistic ideas and the development of technological ideas. Cunningham said:

> [The work of James Joyce for example] goes from paragraphs, to sentences, down to words – and now to words themselves separated, so you don't have even a whole word, you just have part of a word. And that is quite apparent – and seems to me quite reflected – in our technology. That doesn't mean that they [Joyce, Eliot, etc.] did it because of technology. It just happens that those ideas are in the air. Technology is full of this... the electronic system where they cut things so fine... you get it on television all the time.[32]

Merce Cunningham, who has been using chance procedures in making dance since the early 1950's, also incorporated these procedures when creating movement with the computer. For example, many of Cunningham's movement sequences created in LifeForms determined how the body would move, what body parts would be used, or what physical shapes would be incorporated by the use of chance procedures. When these movement sequences appeared physically impossible, Cunningham worked with his dancers to discover how they could be made to work. Cunningham has said: "If a dancer tells me that something won't work, I say, Try it; if you fall down, you'll find out something about falling down"[33].

The Use of Chance Procedures in LifeForms

When Cunningham talks of his work with LifeForms he says, "Like chance, [LifeForms] prompts me to think, well maybe there's some *way* to do that that I hadn't thought of."[34] For example, in *Trackers* there was a structuring of what categories of movement material would be used, decisions about continuity (which movement element followed the other, and what length of time the movement would take), and also construction of the movement material itself. All of these were derived using chance procedures.

Just as Merce originally used chance to thwart his own physical habits, he uses it now to undermine the control of he-who-wields-the-mouse: he'll often

---

[32] *Ibid.*

[33] Joseph H. Mazo, quoting Merce Cunningham in "Quantum Leaps", *The Record*, Bergen Country, New Jessey, 15 March 1992, p. E-8.

[34] Deborah Jowitt, quoting Merce Cunningham in "He Who Wields The Mouse", *The Village Voice*, New York, 17 March 1992.

toss coins to decide what limb the LifeForms figure will move next and in what direction.[35]

Comments from the Cunningham dancers while learning some of the more complex LifeForms phrases have noted an increasing complexity reminiscent of Cunningham's early work with chance. Alan Good, a dancer with the Cunningham Dance Company, has said of this process, "... but [Merce] liked that. So here we were doing this [computer generated movement] .... I mean to change those years of training, ... it was like you were drawing a straight line in a curved universe, it was very difficult"[36].

Sequence Generation in LifeForms

Since Cunningham has never been interested in a singular methodology for creating dance without the computer, it is not surprising to find variety in his approach to creating sequences with the computer. The examples illustrated here are from *Trackers*, Cunningham's first dance created with LifeForms. One method Cunningham used to create sequences was in selecting existing stances through chance operations and then chaining them together (Figure 5). A sequence entitled "CKExitStances", in the *Trackers* LifeForms computer menu is illustrated below. The fifteen stances which comprise the sequence were danced by Chris Komar.

Another method used by Cunningham to generate movement in LifeForms is selecting existing sequences found through chance operations. An example is the movement phrase entitled "Cart 2", a series of two cartwheels shown in Figure 6.

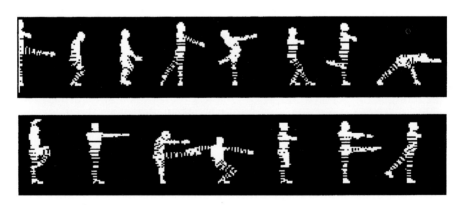

Figure 5   CKExitStances selected by chance procedures.

---

[35]   Deborah Jowitt, "He Who Wields the Mouse", *The Village Voice*, New York, 17 March 1992.

[36]   Alan Good, interviewed in *The Late Show*, New York, 17 April 1992, a BBC television interview with Merce Cunningham. Thecla Schiphorst, and Cunningham dancers: Alan Good and Emma Diamond. Aired August 1992.

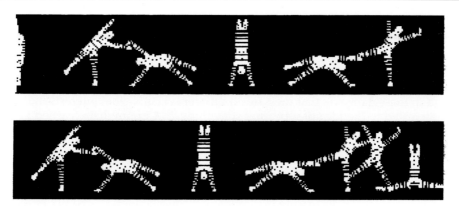

Figure 6 Cart2, existing sequence selected by chance.

This phrase was performed in *Trackers* by Jenifer Weaver. Merce Cunningham has said of using this method in LifeForms:

> In working out something, particularly using chance means with the LifeForms system, I try not to make any decision about whether I like it or not, or some idea like that, or even, whether it is possible, but rather, to look at it and see, oh, that could be possible under certain circumstances, and it is in that sense, the same as when I began to work with chance operations years ago.[37]

In *Trackers*, Jenifer Weaver entered from downstage right, while a second dancer, Robert Swinston, ran from upstage centre to support her so that she would not fall over during the lean to the left. This is an example of Cunningham's ability to look at the phrase, as it was "found" in LifeForms, and then find circumstances that would allow it to be performed in a way that remained as close to its original representation as possible. The result is an often unexpected and surprising juxtaposition of movement ideas that continually provide a mechanism for unforeseen and often startling, or in this case, even humorous relationships to unfold.

A third method Cunningham used for generating movement in LifeForms was to create sequences through learning to use the system. For Cunningham, the learning process has been an ongoing one, not only in learning to use LifeForms, but also historically in continually searching for new ways of creating movement and understanding dance.

> I still do it because it [making dances] interests me. What's exciting is when I come across an idea that I'm unfamiliar with, or when I have a question to answer for myself. You have to find a way to do what you can do. It is

---

[37] Merce Cunningham quoted in the BBC television series, *The Late Show: LifeForms and Cunningham*, broadcast June 1992.

difficult for all of us, but if it's something that interests you deeply, you will find a way.[38]

Cunningham's fervent interest is in finding new ways of understanding elements of movement, not in rehashing or reiterating what he has already done. In talking about the dances he has made with LifeForms he has said: "The common thread in these dances is that they are all different. That's what interests me. I am not interested in the idea of repeating something."[39] Cunningham learned to use LifeForms both during tutoring sessions and in time spent with his own experimentation. One important characteristic that exists in the way that Cunningham has used the LifeForms system is a certain lack of distinction between what he created as learning exercises for himself, and what he created for his dance pieces. Making dances for Cunningham is fundamentally about learning and questioning. It is therefore not surprising that much of the movement created in LifeForms has found its way into his dances. Cunningham has noted that even the earlier stance-based version of LifeForms was used to generate certain shapes or stances that appeared in earlier works such as *Polarity* (1990). An example illustrated below in Figure 7, "Leaper" was constructed originally as an exercise in learning how to cause the LifeForms figure to jump, and then change direction in space. The movement phrase "Leaper" was performed in *Trackers* by Helen Barrow, Robert Swinston, Carol Teitelbaum, and Jenifer Weaver about one minute into the dance.

Figure 7   "Leaper" Sequence created learning to use LifeForms.

Another method used by Merce Cunningham is the creation of new movement in LifeForms using chance operations. Cunningham used chance to select which limb would be moved, how many limbs would be moved simultaneously, and what types of movement the body moved through. The Apsaras phrase seen at the beginning of *Trackers*, at approximately 1 minute and 30 seconds into the piece was created in this way. At this point, Merce Cunningham and Jenifer Weaver are in the upstage right corner, and both support each other in performing the phrase (illustrated in Figure 8). First, Cunningham holds Jenifer Weaver while he turns her on the spot as she executes the phrase, and then Cunningham who is on the floor on his knees, remains there while performing the phrase while Jenifer Weaver turns Cunningham around in a complete circle. Each dancer takes turns supporting the other while the supported dancer performs the Apsaras phrase.

---

[38] Thomas B. Harrison quoting Merce Cunningham in "Cunningham: Choreographer devises movements on a Computer", *Anchorage Daily News*, February 23, 1992.

[39] *Ibid.*

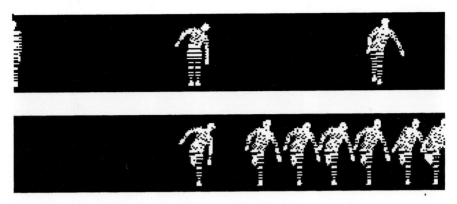

Figure 8   Apsaras phrase created with chance procedures.

One of the details worth noting in this Apsaras phrase is that the time relationship between the stances or shapes created is uneven or unequal. This produces movement that does not have a sense of metered rhythm, but rather has an uneven rhythm which is an artifact of the length of the spaces inserted between the shapes produced by Cunningham. It was this ability of LifeForms to allow a more arbitrary time relationship to exist between specified physical shapes, rather than having to define any particular timing or meter, that appealed greatly to Cunningham. This was what Cunningham was alluding to when he said. "Working with LifeForms suggests possibilities of working with time and space that I had never thought of before"[40], and also when he said, "Things can happen that you think are impossible, but if you try them out, they lead you to something else. And it's all in space, not time, you're looking visually and putting things in space."[41] This is not to say that a choreographer couldn't define movement very specifically based on exact counts or points in time if she chose to do so; but it is not necessary to build movement that is specially time-based using LifeForms.

Cunningham's method of creating movement in much of the work he has created reflects an approach that is not concerned with thinking about the specific timing while the movement is created. Once it has been created, however, the rhythms produced are often complex and polyphonic, using different rhythms in different parts of the body. Cunningham always attempted to remain true to what was produced with his particular chosen method of creation. One of the striking observations of movement created without an effort to define specific timings, is that the outcome has an inherent rhythmic complexity which would be difficult to consciously create in a single iteration.

Finally, one last example of Cunningham's diversity in generating movement in LifeForms, was adding to or modifying existing locomotor patterns such as a

---

[40]   Anne Pierce quoting Merce Cunningham, in "Cunningham at the Computer", *Dance/USA Journal*, Summer 1991, pp. 14–15.

[41]   Jennifer Dunning quoting Merce Cunningham, in "Dance by the Light of the Tube", *New York Times Magazine*, March 1991.

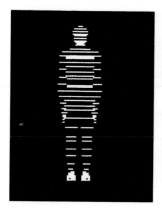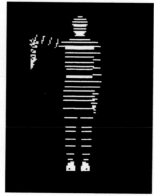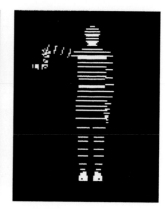

Figure 9   Apsaras showing selection of limbs: shoulder, elbow, and hand.

simple walking pattern, again using chance procedures. This was used in the *Walker* phrase, which was performed in *Trackers*, at approximately 16 minutes into the piece, first by Helen Barrow, and then joined by the dancers Kimberly Bartosik, Michael Cole, Emma Diamond, Emily Navar, Randall Sanderson, Robert Swinston, Robert Wood, and then finally Chris Komar. *Walker* was constructed in three separate iterations. During the first pass, Cunningham used a walking pattern which existed in the LifeForms menu, and began to alter the timing of the walking step pattern, by simply increasing or decreasing proportional timings between steps (see Figure 10, 11). It is this ability to increase the spatial proportion between shapes in a direct visual way that leads Cunningham to say "instead of thinking in time, you're looking visually and putting things in space."[42] In this first iteration, the effect of increasing the spatial relationship between walking steps directly affected the timing of the steps causing a quirky, uneven, and distinctively odd walking rhythm.

During the second iteration (see Figure 12), he added the arms without referring to any relationship between what was occurring in the legs. Again, this immediately created a complex polyrhythm in the body with legs moving irregularly, and then arms moving in their own irregular rhythmic pattern and shape. In the third iteration, Cunningham added the torso and head to the phrase, again without reference to what was occurring in the legs and the arms. The result of this procedure was a walking phrase which was highly idiosyncratic, and was reported by the dancers as very difficult to learn because of its sense of going against what the body naturally did when it walked. Again, it is striking to note that Cunningham created such an iconoclastic walking phrase by beginning with a regular and "normal" walk cycle which was originally placed in LifeForms to provide natural-looking walks which are difficult to animate or generate with a simple keyframing approach.

It is this tendency of Cunningham's to look at both the movement that existed

---

[42]   T. Massari Mc Pherson quoting Merce Cunningham in "Mentor of Motion", *The Anchorage Times*, 23 January 1992.

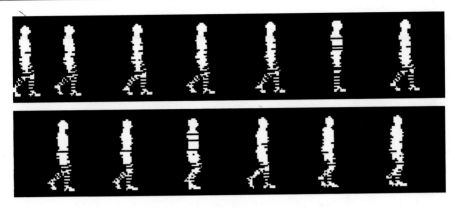

Figure 10   Walker phrase: original walking step.

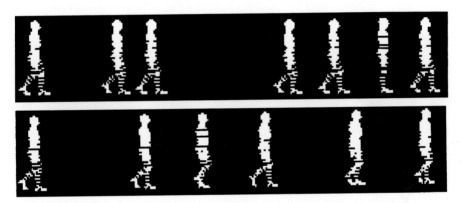

Figure 11   Walker phrase: Iteration 1, create walking rhythm by inserting space between each walk frame.

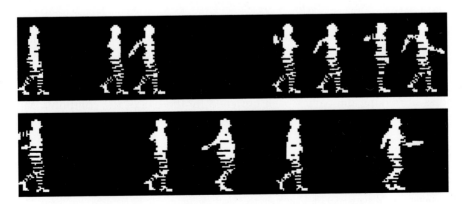

Figure 12   Walker phrase: Iteration 2, create arm movements.

in LifeForms and the operational features of the LifeForms system, and then find new and fresh ways of combining them rather than to try out what LifeForms was "supposed to do." It is an approach that looks beyond the defined boundaries, and continually attempts to break the standard rules which are rendered arbitrary when viewed from this perspective. Cunningham, who calls himself a practical person, is able to create specifically with what exists while simultaneously rethinking the very material with which he is working. Cunningham has commented. "My point about working with LifeForms is not to complain about what it can't do, but to look and see what it can do."[43]

Summary

> In one way or another what we thought we couldn't do was altogether possible, if only we didn't get the mind in the way.[44]
>
> Merce Cunningham

The increase in public awareness that has resulted directly from Cunningham's use of the computer has infused and penetrated current thought while it has simultaneously changed the face of dance. It is directly through the dances he makes that Cunningham has amplified the understanding that choreographers can work with computer technology to extend possibilities in creating dance. Cunningham continues to be a mentor and inspiration to generations of dancers and choreographers. When Cunningham initially began his work with LifeForms on the computer in December 1989, public response to this new exploration was to treat it with curiosity, but still somewhat skeptically. As Cunningham's experience and ability to use the software has grown, so has his experimentation with the system in creating dance. In the few short years since Cunningham has been using the computer, the response to this prospect has moved forward with renewed interest, acceptance, and a willingness to explore the possibilities that could result from this intersection of disciplines. Dance reviewers and critics write about his new work, describing how they imagine he could be using the computer to create dance:

> In *Change of Address* six dancers fall to the floor, legs pretzelled, and lie there tipped at odd angles. I imagine him pressing keys and coming up with something that leaves the dancer with no leg to stand on.[45]

Dancers have been enlivened with new ways of working, and the creative process of making dance has been enriched by the use of the computer. Merce Cunningham's work with dance and computers has shown that not only does the

---

[43]   Jody Leader quoting Merce Cunningham, in "Cunningham's computer-assisted dance comes to UCLA", the *LA Daily News*, 9 May 1991.

[44]   Cunningham, Merce (1985) *The Dancer and the Dance: conversations with Jacqueline Lesschaeve*, Marion Boyars Publishers, New York, London, 1985.

[45]   Deborah Jowitt "Wildfire", *The Village Voice*, New York, 7 April 1992.

technology grow in response to the choreographers that use it, but that the choreographic process also grows, is enlarged and responsive its use. The design and creative process is symbiotic, and the design of LifeForms, and the design of the dances created with LifeForms affect one another deeply[46]. This relationship between objective and subjective has been noted in Cunningham's work; in April 1992, Joan Acocella wrote:

> The most striking characteristic of [Cunningham's] work, aside from its formal beauty, is its objectivity. No dancing on the American stage today is freer of sentimental pretension... And, by a familiar paradox, this objectivity gives [the dancers] a huge subjective force... The two new works, *Change of Address* and *Beach Birds*, were both marked by a rather strange mix of greater literalism and greater obscurity than one is used to seeing... In 1990 Cunningham started using a computer as an aid in composing his dances. These two opposing developments may account for the oddly literal and oddly counterliteral quality of the new works. Thesis, antithesis.[47]

Another review of the dance *Enter*, premiered at the Paris Opera in November, 1992, responds to the idea of "Cunningham's obsession with technology" by speaking of the relationship between the parts and the whole, describing Cunningham's "dissection" of the human body, and the resulting "masterful" dance work:

> *Enter* is the brainchild of Cunningham's obsession with modern computer technology... Cunningham dissects the human body with a computer mouse, breaking down the simplest gesture into composite parts... The title *Enter* is no accident. It was inspired by what Cunningham called "the most important button" on the keyboard... Theatergoers and Cunningham admirers loved it. So did the critics, who hailed the hour-long creation as his finest achievement: "all of his contributions to modern dance are so masterful, so glorious that *Enter* is the culmination and crowning of his life's work."[48]

Merce Cunningham's ability to work in new ways while capturing the public imagination is due in part to his attitude of looking beyond the preconceptions that limit our ability to attempt unlikely combinations of movement, or of movement tools. This viewpoint has been a part of Cunningham's work in dance for over fifty years. Cunningham has paved the way for others to explore LifeForms as a choreographic tool, and has done so by continuing his quest to understand and create movement beyond the limitations of imagination. As Cunningham has said, "You have to find a way to do what you can do. It is difficult for all of us, but if it's something that interests you deeply, you will find a way.[49]

---

[46] Calvert, T.W., Bruderlin, A., Mah, S., Schiphorst, T., Welman, C., "The Evolution of an Interface for Choreographers", *InterChi Proceedings*, InterChi Conference, Amsterdam, April 1993.

[47] Joan Acocella, "Merce Cunningham Dance Company", *Financial Times*, 28 April 1992.

[48] Marilyn August, "High-Tech Inspires Choreographer Cunningham at 73", Associated Press Writers, Paris, October 1992.

[49] Thomas B. Harrison quoting Merce Cunningham in "Cunningham: Choreographer devises movements on a computer", *Anchorage Daily News*, Sunday 23 February 1992.

Acknowledgements

The author gratefully acknowledges Merce Cunningham, David Vaughan, and Michael Bloom at the Cunningham Dance Foundation in New York City, and Dr. Thomas Calvert, Director of the LifeForms Design Team, and of the Center for Systems Science and the Computer Graphics and Multi-Media Research lab at Simon Fraser University. LifeForms has been funded in part by the Social Sciences and Humanities Research Council of Canada. LifeForms interactive motion capture has been funded in part by the Media Arts Section of the Canada Council.

Choreography and Dance, 1997, Vol. 4(3), p. 99–104
Photocopying permitted by license only

Dance on Film: Notes on the making of CRWDSPCR

Elliot Caplan

Figure 1 Merce Cunningham and Elliot Caplan working on "Cunningham Dance Technique: Intermediate Level," 1987. Photo: Erica Lansner.

Caplan, filmmaker-in-residence for the Merce Cunningham Dance Company since 1983, describes the genesis of a documentary film focusing on the creation of a new Cunningham dance, CRWDSPCR, and the life of the company during the rehearsal period. He also defines the principles underlying his work with Cunningham on dance films and videos.

KEY WORDS   Cunningham, film, video, process

I have worked as the filmmaker-in-residence for the Merce Cunningham Dance Company since 1983. My association with Cunningham began in 1977 as a cameraman and production assistant to Charles Atlas, who was the filmmaker at that time. Since I have been the filmmaker, my work with Cunningham has included a series of dancefilms and videos, two educational programs, and a feature-length documentary detailing his fifty-year collaboration with composer John Cage.

It is not my custom to speak about a film before it has been finished, though for the purpose of this article I will attempt to illustrate a few of the ideas that have influenced me during the production of our new film, "CRWDSPCR" (pronounced "crowd spacer"). Completion of this film is scheduled for the fall of 1996.

Those familiar with our work are aware of the use of the camera as an integral part of the choreographic construction. We do not document stage dance, but rather take the dance away from the proscenium and, taking into account the properties of the camera lens, make the dance anew for film and video. The idea of choreographing specifically for the camera is not new. There are entire festivals based on this concept. However, few choreographers have committed themselves to

Figure 2   Elliot Caplan working on *Beach Birds For Camera*, 1991. Photo: Lawrence Ivy.

making this kind of dance for the camera in the way Cunningham has. That commitment has included a full-time filmmaker on staff for the last twenty-five years. This ongoing collaboration of film and dance has resulted in a body of work which traces not only Cunningham's development as a choreographer, but many of the ideas that have shaped the field of filmdance.

Before my training as a filmmaker I studied painting. Both as a painter and a film maker, I was trained to see. Many of the ideas I learned in painting carried over to film. Issues of light, color, composition, placement, and weight still guide my work. When dealing with these issues, I work with the film screen as a canvas. I sometimes think of myself not so much as a filmmaker, but as a painter who makes films. In the beginning, because Merce's work was new to me, I treated the dance as visual information in front of the camera. After a couple of years photographing the dance, I began to work with him in new ways, suggesting alternatives having to do with format, design, lighting, and editing in order to make the dance as clear as possible while presenting something new, I have always considered the clarity of the choreography, from the viewer's perception of the dance, to be paramount. I also look for details in the dance, in both shooting and editing, to guide the direction of the film.

I remember a story I heard from the filmmaker Stan Brakhage while studying the film with him in Chicago. One evening while he was editing, a strand of film rustled in a nearby bin. Responding to the sound of the movement, he went to the bin, removed the strand of footage and cut it directly into his film. This

Figure 3 Merce Cunningham and Elliot Caplan working on *Points in Space* (1986). Photo: Robert Hill for BBC.

revolutionized my thinking about film as well as artistic process. I didn't start listening for the rustle of film, though I did begin to pay attention to details in my footage with a new eye.

One of the ways I apply the notion of process in filmmaking is by taking advantage of details that occur behind the main action both in picture and sound. These are found, unpredictable occurrences occupying the same frame as carefully rehearsed scenes. In film as opposed to the stage, small details of movement are perceptible to the viewer. These details can be a dancer's hand moving or the twitch of an eye which convey their own rhythms and when seen become part of the overall experience of the dance. I look for these events and accent them as a way to exaggerate movement and convey choreographic ideas. Matisse often spoke of the necessity of exaggeration in painting to clarify a visual idea, and I have found it to apply to filmmaking as well.

Following the making of "Beach Birds For Camera", Cunningham and I spoke of a new film which would portray the atmosphere and feeling of the working dance studio. We would turn the camera on ourselves and document the process of making a new dance. In this case, the new dance would be "CRWDSPCR". Merce was continuing to choreograph with the help of computer software designed to track and record movement combinations put into it. Because of both time and money restrictions, the regularly scheduled afternoon rehearsal with the dance company became the time we would make "CRWDSPCR". Despite the restrictions, however, the most important thing to me is to do the work no matter what the budget.

We used a small documentary crew in our own studio, little or no set lighting, and filmed a little every day of what seemed interesting. The camera would go everywhere, all aspects of our working lives within the dance company would be open to filming, such as the dancers working out their movements in spaces other than the main studio. The idea was to "profile" common daily activities within particular situations and watch them unfold over time; included would be development of the piece through rehearsal, costume preparation, Cunningham working out movement from computer to dancer, and the ideas behind the design and music. I had explored this way of working in an earlier film, "CAGE/ CUNNINGHAM", which also featured simple, daily actions mixed with segments from finished pieces spanning fifty years of work. In that film, actions such as watering plants, walking down a street, and cooking helped to create a portrait of who these men were. I like the everyday. It is the most familiar and the most overlooked. It has served me well. Pre-production of "CRWDSPCR" was brief. A crew was assembled, a budget and schedule drawn up and, shortly after, filming began. Merce seemed unusually impatient to begin.

I hired a cameraman who had never shot dance before. This situation interested me because of his documentary skills. We began by discussing the issues of filming dance, watching company class, and looking at the films I had already made. I spoke with him about the sense of weight a dancer displays when moving and how it might help him, without remembering a particular phrase, to be able to see where the weight placement was and allow that to guide his camera frame. Given the physical limitations with reference to weight placement, the frame line of the camera can be fixed on a dancer since the position of that dancer is within certain limits. I imagined an experienced documentary cameraman would readily understand such a concept, accept it, and use it. He did. We had enough money for only one week of shooting.

I like to film dance in a variety of spaces because it expands the possibilities for editing. Following discussions with Merce about filming him at his computer, it occurred to me that the computer's output, the monitor screen, could be used in our filming process as an additional space. This idea of accessing electronic images was not new to me, but the utilization of the monitor screen as a dance space was new. During editing, this will open up changes in tempo and speed of sequences which I can then alternate with actual rehearsal footage. We recorded the dance from the beginning of the dancers' learning the steps to near the end when they were able to perform the entire piece, but before the movement was ingrained in their muscles – the final stage that occurs only after several performances. The visual material of the dancers learning the steps was especially wonderful because of the awkwardness not usually displayed by trained dancers. The choreography in this dance was especially difficult in terms of rhythm and speed of execution, thus allowing for an extended learning process. We had various conditions of weather, but since it was June, the windows were always open. This would be our summer film. So we thought, until shooting was extended through the following winter. The film then became also a portrait of the changing of the seasons as seen through the quality of light in the main dance studio.

Figure 4   Jenifer Weaver, Frédéric Gafner, and Jean Freebury in *CRWDSPCR*. Photo: Rebecca Lasher.

Merce and I wanted to record the finished work in the studio where the steps had been learned instead of on a stage. The dancers wore costume and, as in all our films, the music will be added later, allowing for the sound of the dancers' footfalls and breaths to be recorded. The editing also took place over a number of seasons, as we pieced together a week, sometimes days when there was money to advance the project. The interesting note about the editing was really that despite its cumbersome finishing, the process largely remained open, which was not always easy. The pressure to "educate" was always present, both administratively and financially. Our interest was not to educate, but to reveal clearly the process of learning. As always, the viewer is presented with a number of possibilities and then is able to perceive these possibilities in a variety of ways. This makes the film-watching experience more active and allows for the possibility, when one sees the work again, to also see it new. It is interesting for me to relive in my mind the process of making the film. No two films seem to occur in the same way and that is also fortunate. But the basic principle I try to work by is to allow the footage to be the guide as to where the film should go. This approach is to me the most real, practical, and tangible way to think about this process.

I have found that when I work with Merce, we say or think similar things at the same time. It is very exciting when this happens because of how little time we actually spend together. Working with Merce Cunningham, and until 1992 with John Cage, has given me the opportunity to bring a personal vision to their aesthetic which now constitutes its own body of work, and which continues to surprise and challenge those who see it. My association with Cunningham now spans nineteen years and we are, for lack of a better term, "used to each other." I have seen his work go into my work and within the last few years I have seen my work go back into his work. It is not that we work in similar ways, because I do not make films "by chance," but we have a shared overall sense of how to approach a series of ideas within a particular period of time of working. These ideas with which we work jump ahead of one another, meet in a similar place for a breath or two, then continue on in separate ways.

Elliot Caplan
January 1995

Choreography and Dance, 1997, Vol. 4(3), p. 105–106
Photocopying permitted by license only

Notes on Contributors

Joan Acocella writes about dance and other arts for *The New Yorker*, *The New York Review of Books*, and other magazines. She is the author of *Mark Morris* (1993).

Elliot Caplan is filmmaker-in-residence at the Cunningham Dance Foundation. He collaborated with Merce Cunningham on *Deli Commedia*, *Points in Space*, *Changing Steps*, and *Beach Birds For Camera*. His documentary portrait, *Cage/Cunningham*, was awarded the prize for Best Documentary at the 1992 IMZ Dance Screen Festival in Frankfurt. *Beach Birds For Camera* won the Grand Prize at the 1993 IMZ Festival, as well as the Grand Prize at the New York Dance On Camera Festival, 1993, and the Grand Prix International Video Dance, Stockholm, 1994.

Marilyn Vaughan Drown has a Master of Arts Degree in Dance History from the University of California. She teaches dance at Crafton Hills College and practices Zen at the Zen Center in Los Angeles. She has published a report in *Dance Research Journal* and is currently working on a screenplay.

William Fetterman was educated at Muhlenberg College and at New York University, where he received his Ph.D. in 1992. He has published several articles on theatre, composed performance poetry, and is the author of *John Cage's Theatre Pieces: Notations and Performances* (Harwood Academic Publishers).

John Holzaepfel is a pianist, pedagogue, and musicologist. He studied piano with Ellsworth Snyder, who nurtured both his interest in contemporary music and his devotion to the piano-playing of earlier times. He also studied with Todd Welbourne at the University of Wisconsin, where he took his undergraduate degree in piano. He has given recitals of music from the 18th to the 20th centuries, and has published articles on medieval and contemporary music. He received his Ph.D. in historical musicology from the City University of New York, where he wrote his dissertation on *David Tudor and the Performance of American Experimental Music, 1950–1959*.

Gordon Mumma was a composer and performer with Merce Cunningham Dance Company from 1966 through 1972. He was a co-founder of the now-historic ONCE Festivals of Contemporary Music, and has collaborated with a diversity of musicians, choreographers, visual and theatre artists. He is Professor Emeritus of the University of California.

Nelson Rivera is an associate professor at the University of Puerto Rico. He has curated numerous exhibitions of contemporary Puerto Rican art and has lectured and published extensively on the subject. In addition, he has been performing and directing his own theatre work since 1975.

Thecla Schiphorst is a choreographer, dancer, and computer system designer. She is a choreographic consultant at the Computer Graphisc and Multi-Media Research Lab at the Center for Systems Science directed by Dr. Thomas W. Calvert at Simon Fraser University in Vancouver BC, and a faculty member at the Emily Carr College of Art and Design in Vancouver. She has worked with Merce Cunningham for the past five years exploring the use of computers for capturing choreographic ideas, and during that time has collaborated with Cunningham on the design of LifeForms.

David Vaughan has been associated with Merce Cunningham for more than thirty years, since 1976 as archivist of the Cunningham Dance Foundation. He is the author of *Frederick Ashton and his ballets* (Second Edition, 1999), and *Merce Cunningham: 50 Years (1997).*

Choreography and Dance, 1997, Vol. 4(3), p. 107–109
Photocopying permitted by license only

Index

CHOREOGRAPHY AND DANCE
AN INTERNATIONAL JOURNAL

Notes for contributors

Typescripts. Papers should be submitted in triplicate to the Editors, *Choreography and Dance*, c/o Harwood Academic Publishers, at:

5th Floor, Reading Bridge House	PO Box 32160	3-14-9, Okubo
Reading Bridge Approach	Newark	Shinjuku-ku
Reading RG1 8PP	NJ 07102	Tokyo 169-0072
UK	or USA	or Japan

Papers should be typed or word processed with double spacing on one side of good quality ISO A4 (212 × 297 mm) paper with a 3 cm left-hand margin. Papers are accepted only in English.

Abstracts and Keywords. Each paper requires an abstract of 100–150 words summarizing the significant coverage and findings, presented on a separate sheet of paper. Abstracts should be followed by up to six key words or phrases which, between them, should indicate the subject matter of the paper. These will be used for indexing and data retrieval purposes.

Figures. All figures (photographs, schema, charts, diagrams and graphs) should be numbered with consecutive arabic numerals, have descriptive captions and be mentioned in the text. Figures should be kept separate from the text but an approximate position for each should be indicated in the margin of the typescript. It is the author's responsibility to obtain permission for any reproduction from other sources.

Preparation: Line drawings must be of a high enough standard for direct reproduction; photocopies are not acceptable. They should be prepared in black (india) ink on white art paper, card or tracing paper, with all the lettering and symbols included. Computer-generated graphics of a similar high quality are also acceptable, as are good sharp photoprints ("glossies"). Computer print-outs must be completely legible. Photographs intended for halftone reproduction must be good glossy original prints of maximum contrast. Redrawing or retouching of unusable figures will be charged to authors.

Size: Figures should be planned so that they reduce to 12 cm column width. The preferred width of line drawings is 24 cm, with capital lettering 4 mm high, for reduction by one-half. Photographs for halftone reproduction should be approximately twice the desired finished size.

Captions: A list of figure captions, with the relevant figure numbers, should be typed on a separate sheet of paper and included with the typescript.

Musical examples: Musical examples should be designated as "Figure 1" etc., and the recommendations above for preparation and sizing should be followed. Examples must be well prepared and of a high standard for reproduction, as they will not be redrawn or retouched by the printer.

In the case of large scores, musical examples will have to be reduced in size and so some clarity will be lost. This should be borne in mind especially with orchestral scores.

Notes are indicated by superior arabic numerals without parentheses. The text of the notes should be collected at the end of the paper.

References are indicated in the text by the name and date system either "Recent work (Smith & Jones, 1987, Robinson, 1985, 1987)..." or "Recently Smith & Jones (1987)..." If a publication has more than three authors, list all names on the first occurrence; on subsequent occurrences use the first author's name plus "*et al.*" Use an ampersand rather than "and" between the last two authors. If there is more than one publication by the same author(s) in the same year, distinguish by adding a, b, c etc. to both the text citation and the list of references (e.g. "Smith, 1986a"). References should be collected and typed in alphabetical order after the Notes and Acknowledgements sections (if these exist). Examples:

Benedetti, J. (1988) *Stanislavski*, London: Methuen.

Granville-Barker, H. (1934) Shakespeare's dramatic art. In *A Companion to Shakespeare Studies*, edited by H. Granville-Barker and G.B. Harrison, p. 84. Cambridge: Cambridge University Press.

Johnston, D. (1970) Policy in theatre. *Hibernia*, **16**, 16.

Proofs. Authors will receive page proofs (including figures) by air mail for correction and these must be returned as instructed within 48 hours of receipt. Please ensure that a full postal address is given on the first page of the typescript so that proofs are not delayed in the post. Authors' alterations, other than those of a typographical nature, in excess of 10% of the original composition cost, will be charged to authors.

Page Charges. There are no page charges to individuals or institutions.

INSTRUCTIONS FOR AUTHORS

ARTICLE SUBMISSION ON DISK

The Publisher welcomes submissions on disk. The instructions that follow are intended for use by authors whose articles have been accepted for publication and are in final form. Your adherence to these guidelines will facilitate the processing of your disk by the typesetter. These instructions do not replace the journal Notes for Contributors; all information in Notes for Contributors remains in effect.

When typing your article, do not include design or formatting information. Type all text flush left, unjustified and without hyphenation. Do not use indents, tabs or multi-spacing. If an indent is required, please note it by a line space; also mark the position of the indent on the hard copy manuscript. Indicate the beginning of a new paragraph by typing a line space. Leave one space at the end of a sentence, after a comma or other punctuation mark, and before an opening parenthesis. Be sure not to confuse lower case letter "l" with numeral "1", or capital letter "O" with numeral "0". Distinguish opening quotes from close quotes. Do not use automatic page numbering or running heads.

Tables and displayed equations may have to be rekeyed by the typesetter from your hard copy manuscript. Refer to the journal Notes for Contributors for style for Greek characters, variables, vectors, etc.

Articles prepared on most word processors are acceptable. If you have imported equations and/or scientific symbols into your article from another program, please provide details of the program used and the procedures you followed. If you have used macros that you have created, please include them as well.

You may supply illustrations that are available in an electronic format on a separate disk. Please clearly indicate on the disk the file format and/or program used to produce them, and supply a high-quality hard copy of each illustration as well.

Submit your disk when you submit your final hard copy manuscript. The disk file and hard copy must match exactly.

If you are submitting more than one disk, please number each disk. Please mark each disk with the journal title, author name, abbreviated article title and file names.

Be sure to retain a back-up copy of each disk submitted. Pack your disk carefully to avoid damage in shipping, and submit it with your hard copy manuscript and complete Disk Specifications form (see reverse) to the person designated in the journal Notes for Contributors.

Disk Specifications

Journal name _____

_____

Date _____ **Paper Reference Number** _____

Paper title _____

_____

_____

Corresponding author _____

Address _____

_____

_____

_____ **Postcode** _____

Telephone _____

Fax _____

E-mail _____

Disks Enclosed (file names and descriptions of contents)
Text

Disk 1 _____

Disk 2 _____

Disk 3 _____

PLEASE RETAIN A BACK-UP COPY OF ALL DISK FILES SUBMITTED.

GORDON AND BREACH PUBLISHERS • **HARWOOD ACADEMIC PUBLISHERS**